Killing Sustainability

KILLING SUSTAINABILITY

Blunt Truths about Corporate Sustainability/Social Responsibility Failures and How to Avoid Them

Lawrence M. Heim

Disclaimer: This book presents aspects of and opinions on accounting principles, corporate valuation approaches, investing philosophies and SEC financial reporting, along with related matters. The information contained in this book is not intended as legal, accounting or financial advice and shall not be relied on as such. The author makes no representations or warranties (implied or otherwise) concerning the book's completeness, accuracy or fitness for a particular purpose. The author shall not be liable for any and all loss or other damages, including special, incidental or consequential, or claims thereof. Counsel or advice on the topics covered in the book should be obtained from appropriate professionals. Works by others referenced herein are assumed to be accurate and valid, but were not independently verified by the author unless otherwise stated. Slight differences exist between the print and electronic versions of this publication.

This book was printed through Amazon's print-on-demand process. While the author was unable to select recycled content characteristics of the paper, the print-on-demand process naturally reduces the environmental footprint of this book because no resources are wasted in pre-printing physical inventories.

Contents

PREFACE

Richard Thaler, the winner of the 2017 Nobel Peace Prize in Economics, said in his book *Misbehaving*, "Even for those of us who can't remember where we last put our keys, life offers indelible moments."

Like most people, I've had indelible moments. I recall the moment a voice announced over my high school PA system on March 30, 1981, that President Ronald Reagan had been shot. And I know where I was on Central Expressway in Dallas when my radio blared that former Oklahoma University Football Head Coach Barry Switzer replaced Dallas Cowboys' Head Coach Jimmy Johnson for the 1994 NFL season. Some may not view this event quite as important as an assassination attempt, but for me – a Texan, lifelong Cowboy fan, and a Texas Longhorn – it was a close second.

The date my professional life changed escapes me, but I see the moment in my memory. One dreary day in the winter of 1993-1994, Greg Rogers, a CPA and Associate in Vinson & Elkins' Dallas environmental practice whom I knew from my V&E days, had agreed to lunch. I was a low-level environmental consultant in the Dallas office of ENSR Consulting & Engineering, hoping to persuade Greg to refer business to ENSR. He had a different agenda. He handed me a pre-print copy of *Green and Competitive: Ending the Stalemate* by Harvard Business School Professor Dr. Michael E. Porter and Claas Van Der Linde. Porter is perhaps most well known for his books *The Competitive Advantage: Creating and Sustaining Superior Performance, The Competitive Advantage of Nations* and *On Competition. Green and Competitive* was later published in the September - October 1995 issue of Harvard Business Review, and launched the "Porter Hypothesis" - the theory that stringent environmental requirements catalyze innovations resulting in unexpected value. The Porter Hypothesis remains relevant, and is the basis for much of the literature on environmental economics.

Even though I had worked in environmental compliance almost ten years at the time, this was a new perspective. I read *Green and Competitive* over and over. I covered my copy in yellow highlights and notes in the margin, eventually expanding to a hardbound journal to capture the overflow. New York Yankee catcher and Baseball Hall of Famer Yogi Berra famously said, "When you arrive at a fork in the road, take it." This was my fork, and I took it. Almost two and a half decades later, I am still on that fork.

* * *

This book is not written as a scientific analysis or economic journal publication. A bibliography of key references is provided, but don't look for statistical correlations of data, regression analyses or original survey tools. That isn't the point. Additionally, the information is presented in an informal style. One of my complaints against sustainability professionals is that we tend to make matters overly complex for some reason. I tried to communicate in a simple and clear way.

I hope this is an enjoyable and insightful read.

ACKNOWLEDGMENTS

I gratefully acknowledge the following who played important roles in both my professional development as well as the work leading up to this book: my business partners at The Elm Consulting Group International/Elm Sustainability Partners Patrick Doyle, Joseph Cotier and Robert Bray (using reverse alphabetical order) for their continuous tolerance, trust, support and occasional harassment; Fern Abrams; Dr. Christopher Bayer, PhD.; Hui Chen; Jeff Civins; Cindy Cooley; John Cusack; Commander Kerry F. Gentry, USN (Ret.); Carrie George; Ray Kane; Greg Rogers; my mother (who, as a former English teacher and journalist, read and edited two versions of the manuscript for this book) and late father; my family; and the multitude of folks with whom I have worked, talked and argued.

I also recognize those whose work was important to this book and my understanding of accounting, economics and sustainability/CSR: Joseph Bower, Robert G. Eccles, Paul Griffin, Mozaffar N. Khan, Tim Koller, George Lakoff, Baruch Lev, Michael G. Luchs, William Nordhaus, Lynn Paine, Michael Porter, Per Espen Stoknes, Richard Thaler and Tim Youmans.

Someday, I'd like to meet all of you.

INTRODUCTION

I expect this book to be controversial and incite reaction. Much of what is presented exposes facts, situations and research that stand in contrast to popular thinking about sustainability and corporate social responsibility. There will be those who will attack this book because it threatens their agendas (mainly revenue). So be it. My agenda is about clarity and reality.

From the book's title, anyone would be justified in thinking that I am against corporate sustainability, social responsibility, environmental, health and safety initiatives. The reality is exactly the opposite: I don't want to end sustainability at all – I want it to grow and thrive as part of the global economic engine. But change is necessary from current thinking.

When I began my career three and a half decades ago, the word "sustainability" was not used as it is today. "Recycling" may have been the closest thing at that time. Sustainability initially was about reducing the environmental impact of manufacturing, but at times included community involvement, global impacts, product health impacts, and natural resource extraction. To a large extent, the meaning of sustainability is still in flux.

Corporate sustainability still does not have a generally agreed-upon scope or definition.

Each individual and corporation may define - and defend - it in any way they choose. Any argument can be controlled if the matter is continually defined and redefined by one party.

I make my living advising companies on sustainability and environmental matters. Convincing organizations to end their work in sustainability is definitely not in my self-interest. At the same time, I see companies headed down a path of least value with their existing program or missing out on financially meaningful opportunities by ignoring sustainability due to erroneous preconceptions and myths in the C-suite. That is what should be killed.

What does it mean to kill sustainability? It means to take a hard look at the current sustainability/corporate social responsibility (CSR) plans and kill the behaviors that create unnecessary obstacles to achieving goals. Pursue new avenues, like

- take advantage of human behavior and psychology to influence executive and customer decisions;
- end the use of garbage economics or trying to force value where it may not exist or can't be quantified in a reasonable manner;
- stop using meaningless jargon and buzzwords;
- talk to the intended sustainability audience, whoever that may be; and
- quit using the word "sustainability."

This book is about sustainability failures and obstacles, their origin and avoiding them. My background is in manufacturing sectors rather than power generation, real estate or services. The book doesn't directly address construction, US Green Business Council (USGBC) Leadership in Energy and Design (LEED) systems or sustainable cities, although the principles in the book can likely be applied to any organization. I'm not trying to preach to the choir – those who have figured out how to overcome internal obstacles. My intent is to grow the congregation by recruiting from the outside, convert the unconverted - *small to medium size companies with limited resources and motivation.* This is where the largest untapped potential lies.

For those working in companies that have avoided sustainability/CSR initiatives because of a perceived lack of business relevance, I hope this book will help in finding, designing and implementing opportunities without the usual pitfalls.

CHAPTER 1
WHAT THE HELL IS THAT THING?

Back in the days of the original Not-Ready-for-Prime-Time Players on *Saturday Night Live*, there was a sketch that still makes me laugh. Bill Murray and Steve Martin stood next to each other, staring out into the audience, repeating, "What the hell is that thing?" in different ways, cadences, and accents. This went on for a few minutes without a great deal of variation. Stupid, but hilarious.

Many executives and consumers ask that same question about "sustainability" or "corporate social responsibility."

What the hell is sustainability and social responsibility?

The question seems benign, but the answer is problematic. Buzzwords and catchphrases try to wrap the concept into soundbites, creating additional confusion (more on that later). Rather than giving an answer, this book explores the modern history of sustainability/CSR, illustrating various directions it has gone and can go. Paradoxically, the difficulty in defining sustainability/CSR is exactly what allows it to be molded to a specific setting, so long as it can be defended using appropriate knowledge and tools.

The modern idea of sustainability arose from environmental impacts of manufacturing - waste reduction, recycling, raw materials and local air/water quality. Society sought to balance economic prosperity with long-term assurance of breathable air, drinkable water, and uncontaminated land. Sustainability became the next evolution of environmental management systems. The idea soon expanded beyond manufacturing environmental concerns to include global climate change impacts (i.e., greenhouse gas emissions), working conditions for contractors, philanthropy and community involvement. McKinsey & Co.'s 2017 study on sustainability indicated that the top five sustainability topics today are social issues rather than environmental matters.

Key point: *There is no consensus, clear and actionable definition of sustainability/CSR.*

Looking for a definition creates sensory overload, dizziness and headaches. Typing the word "sustainability" into Google returned over 207,000,000 results one day in November 2017. In 2015, the search returned 150,000,000 hits. In two years, 57,000,000 occurrences of the word were added to Google's brain. How about a book about sustainability? No problem, select from any of the 1300+ books on the topic available from Amazon.

Seeking out expert advice on sustainability/CSR can be equally frustrating. There are organizations, certifications, publications, abbreviations, acronyms, buzzwords, seminars, webinars, other-nars, conferences, reporting frameworks, PowerPoint decks -

all aimed at reducing the ambiguity of sustainability, but those simply worsen the situation by diluting the message and undermining credibility. In addition, simply attending relevant events can be financially daunting as they are frequently expensive. Registration for one conference starts at $2000 for corporate registrants and $2400 for service providers, which is not uncommon. Unfortunately, meetings like this can become pricey self-congratulatory events where newcomers or those from smaller companies are ignored. Moreover, the increased registration cost for consultants inhibits information transfer to smaller companies who typically hire consultants to help with program development.

Media outlets go their own direction as well. Newsweek's annual Green Rankings is well known and widely distributed. However, these rankings reflect only what Newsweek considers key environmental indicators; other social responsibility matters are not included. Regrettably, the magazine uses the words "sustainability", "green", and "environmental" interchangeably in the methodology discussion.

McKinsey & Co. published "How companies manage sustainability" based on research conducted in 2010. The firm received responses from 1,946 executives representing a wide range of industries. Twenty percent of respondents had no clear definition of sustainability. Of those that did:

- 56% defined the concept in two or more ways
- 55% centered around environmental management
- 48% included corporate governance
- 41% included social topics

The numbers confirm the executive view of sustainability was built around environmental matters at that time. A shift has taken place, however. Similar to McKinsey's 2017 findings, a 2017 analysis from KPMG concluded that approximately 90% of Fortune Global 500 now includes human rights - not just environmental or climate change.

In September 2015, the United Nations announced the adoption of the Sustainable Development Goals, or SDGs. The UN SDGs are certainly a credible source for defining sustainability/CSR, but at a practical business level, the SDGs may be overwhelming. There are 17 broad individual goals encompassing poverty, education, gender equality and peace along with others that have more business focus. Each goal then has its own sub-goals, of which there are approximately 200 in total.

As final edits of this book were wrapped up, The World Economic Forum (WEF) published its *10th Annual Global Risks Report.* This report is always interesting and valuable reading. Although the SDGs and the Global Risks Report are presented in different terms, I compared them to identify similarities that could be helpful in connecting the SDGs to specific business matters. Eight of the 17 SDGs correlate to the WEF's risks and risk-trend interconnections; conversely eight of the WEF's 13 most significant global risk trends had a corresponding SDG. This may be helpful, or not – depending on your perspective.

Investment groups/interests are not insulated from this fragmentation. I once sat in on a discussion about the Sustainability Accounting Standards Board (SASB) with some of SASB's major backers on the panel. When I offered that sustainability is still not clearly or consistently defined, the panelists were incredulous. Yet, audience members from investor groups and ratings agencies agreed ambiguity does indeed persist. This agreement may be the only point of consistency about sustainability/CSR across the investment community.

When experts can't agree, everyone else is caught in the middle. A myriad of initiatives exist that marginalize sustainability, splinter the market, frequently compete against and contradict each other and create confusion.

How does a sustainability practitioner convince executives, customers, and consumers of the credibility and value of something with no clear definition? By not being intimidated or limited – there is a lump of clay to form and create without barriers or preconceptions. Define it in a way that is most appropriate, genuine and convincing for a particular setting or company. The pages ahead provide a framework of understanding more than what is typically written about the topic.

* * *

The terms "sustainability," "corporate social responsibility (CSR)" and "environmental, social and governance (ESG)" are used throughout the book. In the real world, these terms are used interchangeably, which is inaccurate. To be perfectly clear, the word sustainability throughout this book is the broadest term relating to a management framework for a variety of topics. CSR is one topic under sustainability that covers what I consider ethical aspects of a company's business operations, supply chain and products. ESG is a relatively new term used primarily by investors to reflect financial impact and measurement of relevant management programs.

CHAPTER 2
AIM TO KILL

I myself am a sustainability/CSR practitioner. When referencing sustainability/CSR professionals or practitioners, I am talking about myself. I've made many "wrong mistakes" as the eminently quotable Yogi Berra said: felt pain and embarrassment of my errors and sought Oracles, Gurus and Wisemen/Wisewomen to find sustainability enlightenment, only to be disappointed. Many others have done the same, becoming frustrated with not making the impact they desire.

To achieve our goals as sustainability/CSR practitioners, it is time to kill sustainability in our organizations.

What do I mean by "killing sustainability?"

It is not putting the pencils down, ending the work, ignoring the issues or giving up. Don't interpret the book title to mean that sustainability/CSR is a failure and unworthy of pursuing. Nor do I suggest lowering ourselves to trickery, greenwashing, false claims or other nefarious activities.

It is about putting the past in the rearview mirror and tackling the issue in a new way, gaining control and continually influencing the issue and its perception. We need to understand why people create barriers, don't accept facts, and how we as sustainability practitioners contribute to these obstacles ourselves. The "old sustainability" needs to be killed to make way for a new sustainability built from the ground up for improved success and impact.

> **Key point:** *One way to begin changing the perception of sustainability is to stop using the word.*

By design, I provide few specific examples. Examples tend to become default thinking and relied on too much. Instead, I set forth principles that lead to a deeper understanding and appreciation of typical obstacles, allowing professionals to navigate by themselves. A sea of articles and case studies is available on sustainability initiatives that were successful in one particular setting. But those examples may not work outside of that company, time or place. My goal is to explain fundamentals so they can be applied to multiple opportunities, not just a single project.

I am aware of the sensitive nature of the title and imagery it may invoke. Even my mother cautioned me. Some may take offense or distort its meaning. To those who find the title and metaphor offensive or distasteful, I am sorry. It is a direct reflection of the book's intent - end the old discourse on sustainability/CSR and use new tools/approaches to help create new conversations.

CHAPTER 3
IN THE BEGINNING

A short history lesson on the beginnings of the US environmental regulatory regime is necessary to understand current obstacles facing broad corporate acceptance of sustainability today.

* * *

From the Industrial Revolution until after the Korean War, US businesses were unencumbered with substantial environmental requirements. After WWII, prosperity in the US crystallized in unprecedented consumerism and manufacturing growth. Waste disposal and air emissions were essentially cost-free and worry-free. US manufacturing was hitting on all cylinders pumping out products as fast as possible. Wars began and ended, each needing provisions and weaponry. New wonder-materials like pesticides, petrochemicals, and plastics developed at a break-neck pace. Prosperity and consumerism were on the rise. US citizens themselves became more (re)productive than ever, manufacturing the Baby Boom generation, which plays a meaningful role in this story.

Heightened social (and altered) consciousness of the Viet Nam war era changed the perception and reality of this growth. A relatively new drug from Germany called thalidomide was intended to treat morning sickness in pregnant women. During the 1960 Food and Drug Administration review for thalidomide approval in the US, the drug was directly linked to severe birth defects. This evidence became public, and FDA denied its approval for use in the United States.

Public concern over new chemicals was awakened.

In 1962, Rachel Carson penned her seminal book, *Silent Spring* on the effects of pesticides on the environment. The book was widely assailed by 800-pound gorillas of the chemical industry – American Cyanamid, DuPont, and Monsanto among them. Even against the headwinds of powerful American corporations, *Silent Spring* found a large audience of open minds, igniting worldwide awareness of new chemicals and their potential dangers.

In 1965, President Lyndon B. Johnson called the Potomac River (which flows alongside the seat of the US federal government itself) a "national disgrace" and *water burned* on June 22, 1969, as the Cuyahoga River in Ohio caught fire.

New social norms, spending power, product availability, manufacturing growth and technological advances conflicted with cultural revolution, concerns of environmental damage, overpopulation and recognition that natural resources are not infinite.

President Richard M. Nixon created the US Environmental Protection Agency (EPA) in 1970. Carson's book is considered to have been a major influence in making that happen. EPA became responsible for administering and enforcing the Clean Air Act (1970), the Clean Water Act (1972), and the Federal Environmental Pesticide Control Act (1972).

Congress added mandates to EPA's mission – chemical registration, waste management, spill control/prevention, refrigerant management and the clean-up of abandoned sites previously used for industrial waste disposal, frequently dating back to WWII and containing a mix of chemicals that would give the Toxic Avenger pause. Each law required a separate set of regulations for compliance, prohibitions, and enforcement.

The "command and control" philosophy of EPA was reflected in the regulations and prosecutory actions. Corporate operating costs, administrative burdens and public pressure rose, as did apprehension.

Prior to EPA, corporate management had considerable freedom from environmental constraints, and the human health/environmental impacts were not seen as a cost. EPA forced companies to face the public's heightened interest in punishing polluters. Disdain for the additional bureaucracy and costs festered in corner offices and on shop floors. Environmental management was deemed a significant non-discretionary expense with no return on investment.

Over the following decades, company leadership transitioned, and the economy transformed. The US position as the world's most important manufacturing center slipped as a global economy took shape. Other countries boasted low operating costs, quietly mentioning the flexibility and simplicity of their environmental regulations - code for "no regulations on the books" or "very limited enforcement." Further, in most developing countries, the working population is not empowered to generate unwanted publicity or obstacles for industrial development. It became the Industrial Revolution and Wild West all over again.

To some back home in America, a global manufacturing economy showed that governmental regulations – specifically environmental regulations – were an unproductive cost dragging down competitiveness of US industry.

Key point: *Like a hereditary disease passed on to next generations of management, contempt about environmental regulations continues to be entrenched in corporate culture.*

Behavioral scientists have given this phenomenon names: arbitrary social tradition, collective conservatism, and pluralistic ignorance. As is discussed later in the book, inertia in business culture is an obstacle to any change, but it can be overcome.

That is the backdrop for corporate perception of sustainability and corporate social responsibility. This plays a far more important part in today's world than might be expected.

CHAPTER 4
AUDITING 1.0

As the environmental compliance burden grew, companies launched audit programs to manage performance in relation to these new requirements. Like other forms of auditing, environmental audits rely on clear and definitive audit criteria. In this case, the criteria are regulatory requirements and permit obligations covering air, water, waste and chemical management. The EPA promulgates these requirements under Title 40 of the Code of Federal Regulations (CFR). Each state then establishes its own requirements based on EPA's.

Auditor knowledge of these technical regulations is necessary, but certain personality traits must be inherent in an effective auditor. Not every environmental compliance professional or engineer was (or is) suited for auditing, which requires "a very particular set of skills," to quote Liam Neeson's character from the *Taken* movie series. An auditor's particular set of skills includes natural skepticism, perseverance, curiosity and the ability to remain objective in assessing facts, applying rules and communicating issues.

Environmental auditing grew into a profession in the 1980s and matured in the 1990s. During that time, increasing pressure for accuracy, credibility and technical competence pushed environmental auditing practices forward. It was not unusual for environmental auditors to be engaged by a company's Board of Directors rather than management, and Boards maintained high expectations. These audits were always carefully reviewed, challenged and questioned, motivating auditors to excel and prepare for the audits and presenting results.

In the mid-1980s, an organization called The Environmental Auditing Roundtable grew from a small group of eight companies to a membership of more than 800 at its peak. The Roundtable became the premier organization for professional environmental auditors, and the meetings were excellent opportunities to get regulatory updates and learn new auditing practices, protocol developments and other related matters. The Roundtable became a central point for professional environmental auditors.

Any discussion of the history of environmental auditing is incomplete without talking about Ray Kane and the firm Arthur D. Little.

Ray is considered one of the fathers of environmental auditing, and responsible for much of the professionalism of EHS auditing today. Ray, along with co-author Lawrence Cahill, wrote THE book on environmental auditing, oddly enough called *Environmental Audits*. He tells the story of writing the first environmental audit protocol on a legal pad while sitting on a plane in the late 1970s. Of course, back then, the volume of environmental regulations was a fraction of what it is today. Ray is fond of pointing out that EPA's regulations have more words than the Declaration of Independence.

Arthur D. Little is a 120-year-old global international consulting firm. During the hey-day of environmental auditing, the firm was the original organizer and sponsor of The Auditing Roundtable, and considered by many to be the pinnacle of the profession. While that characterization may not be shared universally, there is little argument that they brought a level of professionalism and rigor to the practice that did not exist elsewhere at the time. Their auditor training program was seen as the best of its time and still influences many veteran EHS auditors today.

Ray and Arthur D. Little staff supported stringent auditor training curricula and screening. The market agreed, and companies sought an increased level of formalization/recognition. In 1997, the Roundtable, in conjunction with The Institute of Internal Auditors (IIA), launched the first credible environmental auditor certification program - the Board of Environmental Auditor Certification (BEAC). BEAC offers auditor training, education and certifications for health and safety, management systems, the American Chemistry Council's Responsible Care program and process safety management. Ray's training program from the 1980s and 1990s formed the basis of the BEAC training.

Today, environmental, health and safety (EHS) auditing is a mature, well-established profession that has proven to be highly effective. EHS auditing professionals owe a great deal to Ray and Arthur D. Little for that, as well as many others who carried the torch in the early days. The reputation of the profession grew, culminating in 2017 when The Roundtable and BEAC wholly merged into the IIA.

Environmental, health and safety auditing were the first step towards systematizing environmental management, which was itself the first step towards sustainability. New types of audits also grew for sustainability and CSR initiatives in many cases, including EHS topics. The new audits developed their own approaches and standards.

CHAPTER 5
SYSTEMS AS THE SAVIOR

The first wave of environmental regulations plateaued in the 1990s, and environmental auditing headed towards commoditization. Questions arose about how organizations could manage compliance on an on going, and preferably, proactive basis. The international standards for quality systems, known as ISO 9000, were seen as successful – at least by the consultants, auditors and standards-setting organizations. A loud chorus (again, primarily from consultants) rose - build on ISO standards and save the world. Literally.

ISO 14000

The ISO 14000 series of voluntary environmental management and certification standards was born in 1996, and has been revised twice since then. The documents are stuffed with overused and meaningless buzzwords primarily to benefit consultants, auditors and the ISO organization itself. Occasionally, companies implementing the standard also find value. Even so, the standards are an important part of the sustainability journey as they were an attempt to transition from an emphasis on environmental compliance. They focused on policies and management rather than on performance or outcome.[1] Proponents of the ISO 14000 standards argued that once a conformant environmental management system (EMS) was in place, a company would no longer have to worry about day-to-day regulatory compliance because the EMS would provide early detection and prevention of compliance matters.

After leaving consulting for a Fortune 150 manufacturer, I began participating directly in two US groups working on the standards and indirectly in two more. I was initially excited and optimistic about the benefits an EMS could offer. Over time, optimism gave way to uncomfortable realization. The perspective of many participants was an overriding sense of "if we build it, they will come. They will do what we say. If they don't, they are just stupid." In this case, "they" referred to all the world's corporations. Meetings and draft document reviews became pedantic, meaningless and oftentimes little more than a venue for people to show how smart they thought they were. The value of the standards was becoming less clear. It was increasingly obvious that environmental professionals had little grasp of how businesses function and what ISO14001 would require and produce. Expectations created by zealous environmental/EMS practitioners (whether well-intentioned or merely seeking monetary gain) were not met. Management saw this as another example of environmental functions being irrelevant, uninformed and not credible.

---

[1] I am not going to delve into more detail on ISO 14001. For a generally balanced view and analysis of the standard and its consequences, I recommend reading *ISO 14001: A Missed Opportunity for Sustainable Global Industrial Development* by Riva Krut and Harris Gleckman (1998, Earthscan Publications). Although somewhat dated (and covering a now-superseded revision of the standard), the book offers perspectives that remain relevant.

Key point: ISO is still seen by many to be a distraction, with companies generally more interested in hanging a certificate in their lobby than the actual outcome of the EMS.

The ISO 14001 section of the International Organization for Standardization website reflects the way many companies view the standard. The webpage has a picture of a girl hugging a tree and informational brochures that are possibly the single largest collection of buzzwords and jargon on the planet.

EMS Auditing

ISO 14001 requires third party auditing to obtain the EMS certification - the reason many environmental auditing professionals were supportive of the standard. Auditors lined up to become accredited to perform certification audits, but the ISO certification audits were different from the environmental, health and safety compliance audits to which EHS auditors were accustomed. In order to issue an ISO 14001 certification, the auditor did not have to consider the effectiveness of the management system. Rather, the auditor was to assess whether the system contains the elements required of the standard, documentation supporting that, and to some extent whether programs were implemented. A company seeking certification had to identify applicable legal requirements and document their process for doing so and managing compliance, but the ISO auditor did not have to determine if the site actually operated in compliance.

Oxebridge Quality Resources International made an amusing attempt at proving problems with ISO certifications in 2014. They set out to obtain the ubiquitous ISO 9000 certification (the quality management system standard) for a fake company named LifeSink that manufactured concrete life jackets named TruSink. Sadly, Oxebridge successfully found a number of what they call "certificate mills" willing to issue a certificate. A link to Oxebridge's article is provided in the bibliography, and it is fun - yet disturbing - reading. Granted, this did not involve the ISO14001 standard, but the approach to EMS certification was supposed to be the same as for quality, so there is reason to be cynical and concerned.

The June 2013 issue of *the environmentalist* – now called *Transform* - (the journal of the UK-based Institute of Environmental Management & Assessment, or iema) contained a short overview of research on "whether third-party audits of an environmental management system (EMS) could provide sufficient assurance of a firm's legal compliance."

The study determined that "the competence of [EMS] auditors is generally limited to assessing the presence of procedures." Notable divergences exist in the perceptions of how well EMS audits address regulatory compliance. Not surprisingly, 92% of the certification bodies were convinced their audits reflected compliance conclusions very well or quite well. Yet, regulators held a far different view with only 17% saying EMS audits addressed regulatory compliance very well or quite well.

My experience is unfortunately consistent with the regulators' conclusion. One memorable example came after a company completed their ISO 14001 *re*certification audit. The ISO auditor passed the site with flying colors, and was highly complimentary. The following week, I found criminal environmental violations that resulted in the site environmental manager losing his job along with a handful of other repercussions. Sadly, this encounter is not unique. So, what do ISO auditors look at? Paperwork, not the implementation of the paperwork.

> **Key point:** *Assessing the mere presence of procedures is not the same as evaluating the content, adequacy or effectiveness of those procedures.*

Not even close. Unfortunately, problems with audits and auditor performance aren't limited to ISO auditors and extend into sustainability/CSR, as we will see.

CHAPTER 6
BALL AND (SUPPLY) CHAIN

Manufacturers make things and stuff out of other things and stuff made by other manufacturers. The series of business relationships starting from resource extraction (whether that be fossil fuels, metal ores or food crops) to the end consumer - and sometimes a product's afterlife - is called the supply chain (also referred to as the value chain). In the past, companies hiring contract manufacturer(s) and suppliers did not concern themselves with how products were made in their supply chains. Ignorance of what suppliers do, however, is no longer acceptable.

> ***Key point:*** *A manufacturer's influence - and corporate sustainability/CSR - extends backwards into a company's supply chain and forward to a product's disposal or recycling.*

This not only applies to the things and stuff, but also to the people who interact with those things and stuff. Although a deep and wide supply chain is inherent in a global economy, it also obscures visibility and corporate accountability that is increasingly required by customers. Customer pressure on suppliers can be a powerful tool for change that ripples outwards in all directions for better or for worse. Any one supply chain link can choose to change business practices and improve lives. Factories have made improvements in working conditions and environmental management, but there is still a long road ahead.

Sometimes, suppliers only need a slight push to improve, but it is usually more of a fight. Consumer-facing brands or companies subject to public supply chain disclosures implement various tools to identify risks, monitor supplier performance, and try to enforce conformance to codes of conduct. Such changes can also disrupt the business model, pricing and competitive position of both parties, creating a powerful opposing force. Approximately 50% of many companies' costs are the cost of goods sold (COGS) - that is, the price paid for the labor required to make the product, the direct materials used to make the product, and overhead charges necessary for making the product. Sustainability/CSR initiatives can mean increases in all three cost elements.

Key point: Today's manufacturing business model presents the sustainability/CSR professionals' biggest challenge. Manufacturers have minimal influence beyond their direct suppliers and supply chain initiatives. Imposing sustainability/CSR requirements on suppliers can increase COGS.

People

Once hidden from view, the human side of the supply chain is now quite public due to new legislation like Section 1502 of the US Dodd-Frank Wall Street Reform and Consumer Protection Act (2010), The California Transparency in Supply Chains Act (2010), and the UK Modern Slavery Act (2015). These laws require public disclosures of different aspects of the human element in supply chains. Sustainability has its roots in environmental management, but has grown to include social issues (i.e., corporate social responsibility) impacting people in the supply chain:

- laborers digging metal ore out of the earth, bagging and transporting it;
- workers processing seafood and harvesting crops like fruit, cotton, and cocoa;
- artisans dying leather and textiles, sewing them into clothing and accessories;
- technicians assembling electronics and household goods;
- contractors, subcontractors, and employees;
- local, regional and even global communities; and
- customers.

People in the global supply chain face servitude, slavery, human trafficking, abuse of all kinds, substandard wages, exposure to chemicals and hazardous conditions without safety protocols. Some cultures and geographies are sadly defined by these conditions, and many manufacturers take advantage of that. Well-known incidences in the past include those in garment manufacturing, farming, seafood processing and electronics assembly. Look at any consumer product, and chances are workers facing a litany of unacceptable working conditions made it.

As manufacturers identified problems deep in the supply chain, some committed to making changes. This, however, is proving more difficult than expected because a company's ability to influence suppliers/sub-suppliers' fades dramatically as distance in the supply chain increases.

> **Key point:** *A manufacturer can impose contractual requirements onto their direct suppliers, but they must rely on those suppliers to then push requirements/initiatives down further.*

Yet, even direct relationships can be problematic, and that led to a number of new initiatives for holding suppliers responsible for maintaining sustainability/CSR expectations.

Costs are, of course, a major consideration in implementing changes required for customer sustainability/CSR conformance. Especially in the retail sector, vendors are squeezed from every angle to manage costs, and they are not eager to boost wages (or pay wages in the first place) or buy safety gear for workers. Vendors find ways to avoid these costs through deception, fraud, and ignoring facts as we will see later.

In the garment industry, corporate Codes of Conduct launched with the intent of addressing human rights abuses by suppliers. Other industries followed suit. A new cottage industry was created to monitor supplier conformance to the Codes: supplier CSR auditing (covered in a later chapter). Each transparency effort uncovered new concerns and abuses, illustrating the complexity, breadth and depth of corporate supply chains that in some cases, the manufacturers themselves were unaware of.

Things and Stuff Used in Other Things and Stuff

The products we buy usually contain sub-materials and sub-components. Computers and phones consist of thousands of electronic components. Cars, houses, and even garments are likewise made with materials and components made by others. This is a supply chain: each actor in the process of commerce has suppliers and customers. Sub-materials, sub-components and even packaging have social as well as environmental impacts for which brands are being held responsible.

Social impacts of sub-materials and sub-components are covered by the People impacts above, but environmental issues are different. Manufacturing sub-materials, sub-components and packaging generates air emissions, wastewater, and solid wastes requiring management. Consider the boxes used to ship goods ordered online. Trees for the paperboard were harvested, transported to a mill, transformed to pulp and paperboard, which was then converted to corrugated sheeting and the box. That process generates air emissions from log transportation, pulping and converting. Wastewater is generated from pulping and corrugating, and solid wastes from pulping, corrugating and converting. Electronic components are much more complicated with a wider range of environmental impacts associated with their production.

Chemical content of sub-materials and sub-components are yet another important facet. Lead in paint, solder and costume jewelry, phthalates in plastics and formaldehyde in carpeting and wood flooring are examples of harmful chemicals in products. This situation is a triple threat: workers are exposed to the chemicals during manufacturing, customers are exposed during the product's use, and disposal of the product may create another set of problems. These materials are selected by suppliers because they are easy and cheap to get, and in the past, no one checked or cared.

Key point: *The more things and stuff that are made, the more other things and stuff are required - meaning the manufacturer at the end of the line has to invest in understanding and managing supply chain sustainability/CSR.*

Things and Stuff Used Indirectly

Not everything used to manufacture products ends up in the products. For instance, energy is needed for electricity to run production equipment, fuel is needed for transportation and heat, and water is a common resource in many aspects of manufacturing and processing. Even though these are not direct materials, they are still necessary for - and contribute to the environmental impact of - manufacturing processes. For those familiar with CDP, these are Scope 2 and 3 impacts.

Although there tends to be more acknowledgment of environmental impacts of indirect materials, social aspects are still very much relevant. In 2016, a lawsuit was filed against a major US retailer claiming they sold shrimp raised with feed produced by slave labor in Thailand. The suit was ultimately dismissed, but it raised concerns about the provenance of indirect materials. Child labor has been used for years in West

African cocoa farming, especially in Cote d'Ivoire - the world's largest cocoa producer.

Key point: Indirect materials are a component of COGS for manufacturers and their suppliers, and therefore, are not excluded from cost pressure. Sustainability/CSR initiated changes may again impact costs, so resistance is to be expected.

Things and Stuff Discarded

Things and stuff we buy wear out or become obsolete. Sometimes we just want the newest and throw out the old, which has its' own social and environmental impacts. Environmental impacts relate to the disposal of broken, unusable or obsolete products. Social impacts include exposure to chemicals during manual recycling/reclamation activities and the use of slave labor for those activities. To the extent materials are shipped to and reclaimed in developing countries, it is usually a manual process without the benefit of safety equipment like respirators.

Just because technology exists to recycle materials does not mean recycling actually occurs. Vast expanses of e-waste piles in China captured public attention in recent years, and there are now claims that plastic water bottles are exported to India only to sit in their own piles – all ostensibly waiting to be reclaimed in some manner. Most recently, China banned the importation of 24 types of plastics and paper for recycling as of January 1, 2018, saying it no longer wants to be the "world's garbage dump." The ban has already had a domino effect throughout the globe resulting in massive build-ups of recyclables in Britain, Canada, Germany and the US. No alternative has yet been identified to effectively manage the volume of materials previously sent to China. In some cases, recycling is often simply a way of kicking the can down the road.

The enlightened way to manage back-end impacts of disposal is to address them in the beginning - designing products to extend their useful life, minimize hazardous chemical content and reduce post-use recycling burdens. Design for the Environment (DfE) was an initiative US EPA started in the 1990s, primarily in the technology industry. There are four main elements of DfE, but it is useful to expand them for illustrative purposes. These include:

- ease of disassembly, repair, upgrades
- use of recyclable materials
- use of less toxic substances in direct materials
- use of less toxic substances in manufacturing processes
- reduction of packaging
- reduction in product energy consumption

The European Union (EU) End of Life Vehicles (ELV) Directive is a European mandate based on a similar philosophy, but focused on vehicles. ELV bans the use of certain toxic materials in cars, and requires design features to increase recyclability/reuse of parts and materials.

Key point: Current expectations are that manufacturers maintain some level of responsibility through the end of a product's useful life.

It All Starts with Us

Things like computer floppy disks, analog cash registers, old-fashioned photographic film and vacuum tubes were once very much in demand and had supporting supply chains. Today, demand for these items is almost non-existent, along with their supply chains. Each person or organization that buys things or stuff bears responsibility for its demand, and therefore, the supply chain behind it.

As each person or organization comes to this realization, they usually make changes in their behavior or seek product options that are more sustainable or socially responsible. Herein lie business opportunities. Corporate procurement guidelines sometimes give preferential consideration to products that are sustainable or socially responsible.[2] Recent research shows that the next generation of US youth with spending power and coming into the work force (called "millennials") also seem committed to the same buying preferences. Forward-thinking companies will probe these preferences to identify where they can innovate to fill an unmet need. As we will see in pages that follow, innovations like this can result in higher than normal profits.

Key point: Consumption of things and stuff is what creates the need for the supply chain in the first place. This burden can be recast into business opportunity.

---

[2] Examples include grains that are not genetically modified, organic food, products with high recycled content and metals sourced from responsibly-mined ores.

CHAPTER 7
MAKING A LIST, CHECKING IT TWICE

I t seemed natural to extend environmental, health and safety (EHS), and management systems audit practices to reviewing supplier operations. Although a deep and wide supply chain is inherent in a global economy, it also obscures visibility and corporate accountability as we have seen. US concerns about corporate reputation for consumer goods grew after media reports of working conditions in overseas contract manufacturing plants.[3] Labor unions, Non-governmental organizations (NGOs) and others put spotlights on worker exploitation and abuse in factories located outside the US, initially in the clothing, footwear and technology sectors. Multinational companies sought new ways to protect their brand, turning to nascent CSR initiatives to deflect public concern without disrupting their business model.

---

[3] By the way, the US and other developed countries are not completely innocent with regard to poor working conditions and human rights abuses. There have been many instances of abuse, wage disparity, slavery and human trafficking in these countries as well.

Audit Firms

CSR auditing has grown into an industry generating billions of dollars globally, exceeding the value of EHS auditing. One estimate put revenues of the CSR industry at US$80 billion annually. Buyers of these services - typically major consumer brands - frequently select lowest cost providers that may not have appropriate auditing skills or training. Increasing audit time and costs to improve quality or credibility is typically not realistic – the business model of these firms is inherently high-volume, low margin service.

Since the 2000s, social audit standards have been developed and various industry initiatives launched, but their effectiveness has been questioned for several years. John Ruggie, the Berthold Beitz Professor in Human Rights and International Affairs at Harvard's Kennedy School of Government and former Special Representative to the UN Secretary-General for Business and Human Rights said in his Keynote Address at the 2014 Annual Conference of the Business Social Compliance Initiative:

> *"Hundreds of thousands of such audits are conducted each year to ensure minimum workplace conditions in companies' supply chains. Yet exhaustive research has shown that auditing alone has failed to generate sustained improvements in many social performance issues, such as working hours, overtime, wage levels, and freedom of association."*

Ruggie's point is supported by much of the literature on the topic such as the 2013 AFL-CIO report titled *Responsibility Outsourced: Social Audits, Workplace*

Certification and Twenty Years of Failure to Protect Worker Rights. This report investigated numerous CSR industry initiatives, frameworks and audit standards. Findings included third-party audits and certifications based only on telephone interviews without site visits, on-site audits of only four to five hours, and "cursory visits to factories and no proper discussion with workers."

In 2016, Harvard Business School Professor, Michael W. Toffel, conducted three studies into CSR/social auditing by reviewing more than 40,000 inspections conducted in 66 countries. His findings were slightly more positive. Among his key points:

1. Toffel assumed "that most clients want the auditors to tell them the unvarnished truth. Obtaining accurate information from these auditors is critical to enable brands to manage this risk." This is overly optimistic, especially where auditors are hired by factories that have much to lose if audits indicate poor performance.

2. More years of auditing experience and training means a higher number of findings than auditors with less experience/training.

3. Audits are a critical method for knowledge transfer, "and for knowledge to be transferred effectively, you have to have a knowledgeable auditor, but you also have to have a receptive factory manager." The receptiveness of a plant manager is linked to Point #1 above.

4. Audit teams seem to have fewer findings where the factory pays, rather than the brand. Toffel suggests this may be a result of conflict of

interest, but factories are also subject to enormous cost pressures and tend to select lowest cost, less experienced auditors not prepared for complex situations, and well-orchestrated fraud by factory management and workers.

Screening EHS, sustainability, and CSR auditors is a necessary component of getting good audits. One way to evaluate an auditor's background is to get a sense of an average audit engagement. To do this, divide the total number of audits by the total number of years conducting audits to give an average number of audits per year. Then divide that into 2000 (40 hours per week for 50 weeks/year) for the average number of hours spent per audit. If an auditor claims to have completed 2000 audits over ten years, that equates to 200 per year and 10 hours per audit. Or for real workaholics (60 hours per week for 52 weeks/year), this averages 15.6 hours per audit. A determination can be made as to whether that is reasonable for preparation, travel time, on-site evidence evaluation and report writing. For a limited scope audit at a small facility with exceptions-only reporting, this may be adequate. Conversely, it is wholly inadequate in the context of a multi-media EHS audit at a chemical plant, for example.

Key point: Current CSR audit price points are a major driver of audit quality, or lack thereof.

Audit Clients

I have been critical of CSR auditing practices for years, and it is easy to point to the audit firms as the problem. While auditors are complicit, those who buy CSR audit services define the scope/effort and select auditors. In today's CSR audit market, buyers emphasize low cost, commoditize the service and drive out quality while concurrently increasing the scope.

> *Key point: Brands and factories share blame for poor CSR audit quality because they establish scopes, hire auditors and set market prices.*

Fraud is a serious consideration in the supplier relationship and in the context of sustainability/CSR auditing. Audit clients need to understand the potential for and impact of fraud in an audit setting. An article in the MIT Sloan Management Review went so far to say:

> *"It is not uncommon for a supplier to conceal actual practices when a scheduled audit is occurring, or to create a "front" operation for the purposes of the visit. Sometimes, companies discover that a supplier has surreptitiously subcontracted to another vendor that is guilty of various misdemeanors."*

The Fraud Triangle is a useful tool in thinking through fraud concerns in supplier CSR performance.

- **Motivation.** There is much on the line for businesses and their suppliers in terms of CSR results. Disclosures and performance may directly impact revenues, reputation and investor activity.

- **Rationalization.** It isn't much of a stretch to see how an individual can rationalize using alternative facts due to business pressures related to the audit. In some cases, suppliers in developing countries may rationalize their actions further due to their own cultural setting. But let's not kid ourselves into thinking that the US is immune.

- **Opportunity.** There is ample opportunity for motivated suppliers to commit fraud. Those hiring audit firms severely limit the auditors by imposing minimal scope/effort driven primarily by cost. Suppliers know their customers' auditors are not enabled to conduct a thorough review, and with pre-scheduled site visits, they have plenty of notice to dress the place up for the auditors.

Audit clients that identify fraud as an audit risk should engage auditors trained to identify fraud and reconsider other aspects of their approach. Few sustainability/CSR auditors pursue fraud detection education or training that is common for fraud examiners. This training includes interviewing techniques, body language interpretation (doing this correctly requires specific training and skill), document/photo authentication, evidence corroboration and when necessary, forensic accounting. Anyone committed to improving CSR audits procured on behalf of a company should consider the following:

- **Adjust expectations or pricing to match the quality and scope of activities desired.** Be realistic – it isn't possible to drive off in an Aston Martin and expect to pay scrap metal prices. Buying a Yugo doesn't result in getting the reliability and features of a Chevrolet. Auditors are increasingly asked to provide information on topics like structural engineering and local electrical code compliance. These matters require specific technical knowledge beyond that of a typical CSR auditor. Audit scope, expectations, and price must be aligned.

- **Explore the auditor(s) professional qualifications**. Do they hold a relevant third-party certification? How much continuing education is required? Is fraud detection training included? What are the audit firm processes for ensuring the independence of the individual auditors, not just the firm as a whole? Auditors should hold themselves accountable to appropriate professional standards. If they don't, that speaks volumes about their attitude toward their work.

- **Test the auditor(s) technical knowledge beyond checklists**. Does the auditor understand the applicable requirements beyond what is written in the audit checklist or protocol? There are few times when on-site reality matches the auditor's checklist. A professional should apply knowledge objectively and pragmatically, not just check boxes on paper or a screen.

- **Find out how much time the auditor(s) spend onsite, and on each audit activity**. Generally speaking, one day (or less) total on-site is too little for any credible audit scope. An auditor should reasonably balance their time between document reviews, interviews, and visual observations. If inadequate time is spent or there is an imbalance in the activities, make the auditor change their practices.

- **Look at audit report findings and cited evidence.** Is it clear what evidence was reviewed, especially to support findings? Are findings based solely on interviews? While this can be acceptable in some settings/situations, information from interviews typically should be corroborated with another type of audit evidence such as documentation, re-computation/retracing, or direct visual observations. If findings are not based on objective and repeatable evidence, make the auditor change their practices.

- **Determine how audit reports are peer-reviewed, if at all.** All audit reports should go through a formal internal quality check. How are those checks conducted and by whom? Does the review require the auditors' original notes so the reviewer can confirm that the audit evidence supports the findings?

- **Don't get swayed by broad company or program certifications such as ISO.** While these certifications can be an indicator of internal process formalization, understanding the reality of individual auditor performance is far more important.

My private conversations with those hiring CSR auditors indicate that a low level of trust in audit quality exists, concurrent with apathy or resignation that a change isn't possible. Normal practice at this time is for each company to hire its own sustainability/CSR auditors to visit suppliers, meaning that suppliers are inundated with auditors. Audit fatigue at facilities at all points in the supply chain has become an epidemic. I can't count the times I have been at a facility where audits were being conducted immediately before and after - and sometimes during - my visit. Operations are so busy supporting audits there is sometimes little time left over to make the product. I have great empathy for these people.

Thankfully, new developments are emerging to help companies balance cost, audit disruption and CSR management. Available solutions include supplier audit programs sponsored by industry associations where members share the results of a single audit conducted by a third-party firm and supplier ratings as an alternative to conducting audits. Individual companies are evolving other solutions tailored to their own unique situation and customer concerns. To reduce the number of audits at their locations, some companies are considering hiring third-party auditors with deeper expertise and fielding larger, senior-level teams (meaning pricier) and making those audit reports available to customers. The intent is for the supplier to have a different kind of audit that provides both parties higher confidence in the quality, scope and coverage than a typical customer-initiated CSR audit. Although such an audit costs more, it would more than pay for itself in the efficiency gained and reduction of disruption at the facility.

Finally, auditing by itself does little more than check a box (some say it doesn't even do that). To fix problems, problems have to be fixed, not simply found. This was one of Ruggie's points in his statement above. After an audit, the audit client is responsible for implementing and overseeing corrective actions - not auditors.

Key point: *No audit is effective if audit findings are not addressed.*

CHAPTER 8
MAKING FOOLS OF
OURSELVES

T he sustainability profession is its own enemy in terms of how and what is communicated to different audiences. Over the years, some attempts at communicating were beyond reason and at times, simply absurd. As preeminent Texas environmental attorney Jeff Civins says:

> *"There is no common currency in quantifying different environmental sustainability objectives, e.g., water savings versus carbon reduction, and weighing those against each other."*

Without a common basis, language or "currency" as Civins calls it, we sustainability practitioners chase squirrels (another chapter) and make fools of ourselves by how try we demonstrate the value of our efforts, and the way we communicate about sustainability/CSR matters to others.

At this point, a *caveat* is necessary. Portions of this chapter - and others that follow – are slightly difficult (maybe boring is more accurate) reading. Some of that is due to quoted text and some is a reflection of what may be viewed as the dry and technical nature of the subjects. Please accept my apologies in advance.

Maximizing Shareholder Value and Sustainability Valuation

Sustainability professionals have searched for a credible financial metric to quantify the value of our efforts. Only 26% of those responding to McKinsey & Co.'s 2017 sustainability survey reported a positive financial impact of their sustainability/CSR activities, and approximately 25% reported not knowing what the financial impacts or benefits are at all.

For the most part, the sustainability valuation journey begins with environmental management. Like other risk management processes, the value of environmental management is invisible as long as it works correctly: the ROI is not readily quantifiable unless the company also quantifies the financial value of risk reduction, which is uncommon. It doesn't take long for someone to look at cost line items and ask if environmental management costs are necessary. To answer that question, environmental professionals have turned to creative managerial accounting.

"Maximizing shareholder value" (MSV) has been a corporate mantra for decades, and is at least partially responsible for sustainability/CSR creative accounting. Research now shows MSV is really MEPW - Maximizing Executive Personal Wealth.

Various incentives exist to create MEPW rather than shareholder value. For instance, performance-based executive pay above $1 million became a tax deductible business expense in 1992 in the US; almost two-thirds of executive compensation today is in stock. Studies have shown that pay-for-performance contributes to "various misdeeds involving harm to consumers, damage to the environment and irregularities in accounting and financial reporting."[4]

In an excellent analysis of the failure of MSV published by Harvard Business School professors Joseph Bower and Lynn Paine, the authors discussed a difference between creating value for a company and creating wealth for shareholders:

> *"When cash is paid out to shareholders rather than used to fund research, launch new ventures or grow existing businesses, value has not been created. Nothing has been created. Rather, cash that would have been invested to generate future returns is simply being paid out to current shareholders."*

In *Valuation: Measuring and Managing the Value of Companies* (2015), McKinsey & Co.'s Tim Koller offered:

> *"Companies thrive when they create real economic value for their shareholders ... creating shareholder value cannot be limited to simply maximizing today's share price for today's shareholders. Rather, the evidence points to a better objective: maximizing a company's collective value to* current and future *shareholders, not just today's."*

---

[4] More about how pay-for-performance management conflicts with sustainability/CSR is addressed in a later chapter.

Lynn Stout, Professor of Corporate and Business Law at Cornell Law School, called MSV "the dumbest business idea ever." MSV fails for multiple reasons. To begin with, shareholders arguably do not sit at the top of the corporate Mount Olympus. Koller says that past "crises have led many to call into question the foundations of shareholder-oriented capitalism." As Bower and Paine asserted:

> *"...shareholders have no legal duty to protect or serve the companies whose shares they own and are shielded by the doctrine of limited liability from legal responsibility for those companies' debts and misdeeds... public company shareholders have few incentives to consider, and are not generally viewed as responsible for, the effects of the actions they favor on the corporation, other parties, or society more broadly... With few exceptions, shareholders are entitled to act entirely in their own interest within the bounds of the securities laws."*

William Lazonick, Professor of Economics at the University of Massachusetts Lowell further supports the idea that MSV is a fallacy because "public shareholders do not invest in a corporation's productive capabilities; they simply buy shares outstanding on the market, hoping to extract value that they have played no role in helping to create."

Furthermore, reality and theory of the stock market's function don't line up: in theory, companies issue shares in exchange for money to invest in growth. In reality according to Lazonick, "stock markets in advanced countries have in fact been insignificant suppliers of capital to corporations." He states that with MSV as a foundation for executive compensation programs, cash is many times used for stock buy-backs rather than investments in growth/value. Other studies validate Lazonick on this point: an article in CFO Magazine pointed out that:[5]

> *"In 2014, when deposits from mutual funds and exchange-traded funds reached $85 billion, S&P 500 companies poured about six times as much capital, a whopping $553 billion, into stock repurchase programs, according to S&P Dow Jones Indices."*[6]

Even with the cards stacked against the validity of MSV, it persists and perversely compels corporate sustainability/CSR staff to get creative in quantifying the value of their programs and efforts. I was once forced into a misguided and inappropriate implementation of Economic Value Added® (EVA®, trademarked by Stern Stewart & Co., now called Stern Value Management) as part of a corporate cost reduction initiative.

EVA® is a managerial accounting tool intended to evaluate capital investment opportunities and determine if the return on proposed projects exceeds

---

[5] New (2018) tax law changes in the US reduced the tax rate for US businesses repatriating cash located in other countries. Media reports indicate that much of the cash will be used for stock buy backs and employee bonuses.

[6] Interestingly the article's author, Jiakai Chen, takes the position that the problem is not with share repurchases themselves, but because executive compensation is tied to stock price and earnings-per-share (EPS), "management is incentivized to carry out a value-destroying buyback, since buybacks always lead to a higher EPS."

the company's cost of capital and are the best uses of that capital.[7] But in this instance, my coworkers and I had to demonstrate our own personal economic value added by applying the methodology to our everyday activities and expenses. Earlier that year, one coworker found a solution that prevented a shutdown at one of the company's manufacturing locations. He claimed a personal EVA® of $500 million for the year, based on the value of revenue generated because shutdown was avoided, as well as the value of avoided shutdown costs.[8] That is why I call the effort inappropriate and misguided.

In contrast to using empirical formulae (even if they are misused), "environmental risk" is many times a magical concept that can depend on mythical values. To begin with, environmental risk is not well defined. Fines and penalties, spill and contamination clean-up costs, business interruption due to an event, third-party civil suits, associated legal defense costs and the potential for pollution control equipment are obvious aspects of environmental risk. Many of those are insurable risks and are reasonable enough. But what about lost revenues from environmentally related boycotts, damage to a company's brand/reputation, missed business opportunities or projected impacts on stock prices or cost of capital? When I explore these topics in environmental risk assessments, the most common response is either "it won't/can't happen" or "I haven't thought about that."[9]

---

[7] Although Koller doesn't call out EVA® by name, he does mention that a company's growth is "governed ultimately" by Return on Invested Capital (ROIC), which is similar to EVA® but without adjusting for cost of capital.

[8] He wasn't actually serious about claiming this value; he did so to show how ridiculous the corporate mandate was.

[9] An environmental risk assessment should have as its starting point a picture of possible (not *probable*) uncontrolled risks. Once the "gross" risk profile is

In 2015, I wrote an article called *Sustainability is Stupid*. My point wasn't that the idea of sustainability is bad, but that sustainability is too frequently portrayed in a stupid manner in publications, by consultants, and around corporate conference room tables. We sustainability and corporate social responsibility practitioners too frequently also make fools of ourselves.

***Key point**: In our zeal or a need to justify our existence in the context of Maximizing Shareholder Value, sustainability/CSR practitioners overreach; our biases turn into obstacles when we try to force a solution or valuation where one may not exist, or is inappropriate - destroying credibility.*

This bias comes from a myth that sustainability performance is – or should be - always financially material. Materiality in US financial reporting is subjective, which is why there is ambiguity to begin with.[10] The term is not defined so much as it is explained in the 1976 US Supreme Court decision *TSC v. Northway*. The Court stated that in order for a matter to be considered financially material, "there must be a substantial likelihood" that non-disclosure would be "viewed by the reasonable investor as having significantly altered the 'total mix' of information made available." Later in its decision, the Court used the term "reasonable *shareholder*." There are different types of reasonable investors – some have short-term goals and some long-term horizons; others are

---

developed, controls can be overlain to see the net risk profile. Claims that "it won't/can't happen" should be viewed with skepticism and carefully vetted.

[10] Interestingly, in his book *The End of Accounting*, Dr. Baruch Lev chose to address "importance" of information to investors rather than "materiality." Lev apparently wanted to avoid using a regulatory term. More about Lev and his work are in the pages that follow.

interested in dividends, and still others seek limited pricing volatility.

Clearly, there is much room for interpreting who meets the reasonable investor description. Ten years ago, investment decisions based on sustainability were highly unlikely (the advent of new investment philosophies is discussed later). The question about investor use of/need for sustainability/CSR information is now on the front burner.

A myriad of studies dating back to the 1980s have attempted to demonstrate environmental value and materiality in terms of stock price impact or cost of capital. Most of these studies relied on supposed linkages without clear cause and effect, or used meaningless metrics. One study claimed that a company could reduce its cost of capital by 1% by implementing an environmental management system (i.e., from 9% to 8%). Yet no causal connection was demonstrated between the environmental management system and capital costs. As stated in a 2017 study by MSCI, a large ESG investment rating firm, "researchers finding a positive correlation between ESG and financial performance often fail to explain the economic mechanism that led to better performance..."

Recently, three publications realistically linked sustainability and equities valuation. First is an April 17, 2015 letter from the non-profit Ceres to the SEC on climate disclosure. The letter addresses disclosure of climate risk as material information to investors, discussing the matter in terms of asset risk, materiality of future petroleum pricing/demand scenarios, and long-term capital expenditure plans/assumptions for oil and gas companies.

Second, Greg Rogers published a short series of articles analyzing asset retirement and environmental obligations (AREOs), as accounted for under the U.S. generally accepted accounting principles (GAAP) and international financial reporting standards (IFRS). Updates are posted periodically. Greg explains:

> *"Accounting for liabilities is not the same as saving for them. People have trouble planning for retirement, and so do companies. Decommissioning obligations are much like corporate pension liabilities. Complex accounting, measurement difficulty, excessive optimism, and frequent examples of gross underfunding characterize both. But unlike pension liabilities, decommissioning obligations ... cannot be discharged in bankruptcy."*

He unmasks a financial catastrophe facing the oil industry: the growth of alternative fuels, energy reduction initiatives and physical changes in coastal areas where many refineries are located, all of which may force early asset retirements. But meeting legal obligations of AREO values (which Greg states are actually too low) for super major oil companies will require double-digit annual spending *growth rates*. How can companies fund that spending level for the decades required for environmental decommissioning, especially when market conditions are such that operations are shutting down in the first place? Investors don't seem to recognize this long-term uncertainty and cost in the equities valuations.

Third, a working paper by Mozaffar N. Khan, George Serafeim, and Aaron Yoon titled *Corporate Sustainability: First Evidence on Materiality* was published by Harvard Business School. The authors stated that "the prior academic literature has not distinguished between investments in material versus immaterial sustainability issues."[11] Among their findings are that "firms with strong performance on immaterial sustainability topics do not outperform firms with poor performance on immaterial topics, indicating sustainability investments are at a minimum, not shareholder value-destroying." Sustainability topics can be material or immaterial; companies need to determine which is which and don't look to share prices to validate immaterial sustainability efforts.

Not long ago I sat in on a presentation from Subaru of Indiana - the car company's only US plant. The site's sustainability program began in 1994. Back then, they developed a business case for a particular (but quite small) project based on real dollars that was successful. By doing so, they set the foundation for future sustainability initiatives that probably would not have seen the light of day if the business foundation set in 1994 was unsound. On the other end of the spectrum, a 2017 KPMG analysis concluded that while many top 250 companies in Fortune's 2016 Global 500 disclosed qualitatively that climate risk is a potential material risk, a full 97% of the respondents did not use a quantitative method to make the materiality determination. Subaru's initiative was clearly demonstrable but financially immaterial, yet half of the world's largest companies don't even turn on the calculator for a global material risk. That is odd and perhaps, backward.

---

[11] One weakness in the study is its reliance on sector-based sustainability accounting standards that were (and still are) preliminary, unproven, and without consensus on their true materiality.

Koller suggests connecting sustainability/CSR initiatives to cash flow, which is a foundation of corporate value. Cash flow is good: linking it to any sustainability/CSR initiative is valuable financially and builds credibility within the company. This may not be as exciting as talking about the company's stock price, but it is more definitive and the connection is easy to see.

Developing a successful financial valuation may mean temporarily disconnecting any sustainability expertise/bias. Approach the quantification through the lens of company business fundamentals. Don't over-reach or over-sell, but commit to some reasonable methodology. Unless the company already embraces valuations of reputational damage, brand image or avoided contingent risks, don't go there.

Key point: *Linking sustainability/CSR to stock price may not the right approach.[12]*

Finally, another pressure point in sustainability valuation methods has surfaced, especially when the values relate to financial reporting. SEC financial reporting must adhere to Generally Accepted Accounting Principles (GAAP) - a common set of accounting principles, standards and procedures for financial statements. The SEC's Division of Corporation Finance (CorpFin) has become increasingly focused on disclosure of non-GAAP financial measures as well. CorpFin staff commented at a 2017 PLI Securities Regulation Institute panel discussion that they are looking at consistency and

---

[12] For an exceptional collection of current articles covering a range of valuation topics, read the Spring 2017 issue of the *Journal of Applied Corporate Finance,* which is dedicated to "Sustainability and Shareholder Value."

quality of such disclosures. The panelists
recommended that internal controls and policies be
developed to support non-GAAP measures, which may
even require participation by audit committees. Since
no generally accepted accounting principles yet exist for
sustainability/CSR valuations, reporting these values
would be non-GAAP disclosures and should be subject
to the same controls and policies as other non-GAAP
disclosures.[13]

Investors are beginning to question the usefulness of
GAAP information, which may prove to be an
important signal for sustainability/CSR valuation. Dr.
Baruch Lev is a renowned professor of accounting and
finance at New York University's Stern School of
Business. His book, *The End of Accounting and the
Path Forward for Investors and Managers* (2016), offers
a great deal of empirical data supporting his position
that SEC reporting has lost much of its historical
relevance.[14] He notes that GAAP generally reflect
measures based on hard assets like property, buildings,
equipment and physical inventories. However, since
the 1990s, company investments and valuations have
shifted to intangible assets: R & D, patents and brands
for instance. Therefore, GAAP measures are no longer
an accurate representation of corporate performance.

Among the salient points in Lev's research:

• SEC financial reports provide only 5% of the
information relevant to investors;[15]

---

[13] Alan Beller, former Director of CorpFin commented in 2016 that
"sustainability has become the shiny new object *du jour* for CorpFin."
[14] This book should be mandatory reading for anyone working in a publicly-
traded company.
[15] What is relevant to investors, according to Lev, is examined later.

- The number of companies releasing non-GAAP measures to investors doubled between 2003 and 2013;

- Today, only about half of a company's market value reflects earnings and hard asset values, compared to more than 80% a half-century ago;

- Current accounting and reporting requirements count intangible assets as *expenses*, thereby suppressing their value; and

- Reported earnings are now so "contaminated... with multiple nonrecurring, transitory items" that they are of little use to investors.

Other viewpoints on the accounting element include those from John White, a former Director of CorpFin who has pointed out that:

> *"Accountants know how to deal with numbers and things that traditionally fit into ledgers. They bring a great deal of rigor to the disclosure process generally. But that group is not necessarily the group that will be putting together the sustainability information."*

This may seem like a criticism of accountants but it isn't. White highlights the importance of bringing multiple areas of expertise to the table when establishing the value of sustainability/CSR.

Key point: *In the US, traditional accounting and financial reporting measures have become less valuable to investors. Non-GAAP financial disclosures are growing in importance, meaning reported sustainability/CSR valuations should be supported with credible processes, assumptions, and data.*

Saying What We Mean, Or Not

Sustainability professionals are guilty of using overly complicated language that serves no purpose other than to impress others. It is utilized primarily as an intentionally designed technique for obfuscating intricacy of topical coverage relying on a preconceived posit about the audience. In other words, writers sometimes want to prove he/she is smarter than the reader. Read this quote from a recent article:

> *"Thermodynamics is one of the most important bases for working with sustainability, particularly its second law, which defines entropy (in a simple way, wasting energy from a system), and is used in a wide range of fields of study, from economics to ecology. The reason is simple. Understanding entropy implies understanding how one action affects another since the reduction of entropy (something positive) in one system mandatorily causes an increase in another. It follows that a positive activity always has negative results, which must be sought and known to the maximum extent possible."*

This writer is describing a personal characteristic he considers desirable in a sustainability professional. Read the passage again knowing its intended message - does it make any more sense? It is common to find articles containing complicated graphs, charts and formulae along with text written in a thick academic dialect, rendering its meaning incomprehensible. The Working Paper by Khan *et al.,* referenced above unfortunately suffers from this very malady. While fancy words may impart a writer's intelligence (or ego), they may also have no meaning to the reader. Per Espen Stoknes, one of the economists whose work is examined in another chapter, calls this "detaching knowledge from meaning."

Conversely, corporate entities tend to stick to the minimum allowable content in sustainability/CSR reports. These reports are heavily scrubbed by layers of lawyers, frequently say little that is substantive, and in the US, are not usually verified externally. I still find reports with an overwhelming number of empty words in a visually stunning document with pictures of green meadows, forests, and deer.

Then there is the matter of sustainability's unique jargon - its own secret code language. Advertising Age magazine once called sustainability one of its "jargoniest jargon" words. Since then, others have criticized the word's use and its displacement by even more meaningless garbage. Admittedly, I occasionally fall into this abyss myself, especially in the company of other sustainability professionals. Among the worst and most meaningless sustainability buzzwords, some of which have been long embedded in the sustainability lexicon, are:[16]

- Triple Bottom Line
- People, Plant, Profit
- Natural Capital
- Up-cycling
- Circular Economy

---

[16] Lev himself pointed to several of these when describing the "bewildering array of social responsibility concepts, terms, and descriptions advanced by consultants, writers, and NGOs" in his 2012 book *Winning Investors Over*.

- BAU (Business as Usual in the climate change context)
- Earth-friendly, Environmentally-friendly, Eco-friendly, Eco-Efficient
- Return on Resources
- Cradle to Cradle
- Externalities
- Moral Imperative, License to Operate
- Natural, Organic, Green
- Paradigm Shift (using this phrase, in particular, should be punishable by a slap in the face with a dead fish).[17]

Sustainability/CSR consultants are major offenders because we fight to differentiate ourselves in the marketplace. Shiny new services are given catchy names or old ones polished up and renamed in an attempt to capture attention. To be fair, every management consulting firm on the planet is guilty of this, but that doesn't make it right. And doing so is not without risk: the U.S. Federal Trade Commission has published guidance on using sustainability buzzwords for product labeling.

Key point: The question must be asked if the intended audience understands what is being said, and whether they are astute enough to realize what is not being said.

Astrophysicists and Nobel Prize winners write entire books that explain their work simply; why can't sustainability professionals produce reports and articles

---

[17] *Forbes* called this phrase their number one "business buzzword that make[s] you sound way less amazing than you really are" for 2018. *Forbes* is nicer about it than I am.

that are both uncomplicated and meaningful? Two quotes from Albert Einstein are perfectly apropos here:

> *"If you can't explain it simply, you don't understand it well enough.*
>
> *The definition of genius is taking the complex and making it simple."*

Sometimes, using fancy language and buzzwords is just foolish; other times it creates an outright barrier and erodes credibility. Another chapter covers the psychology of executive decision-making and communication approaches for sustainability professionals that maximize chances for success.

Key point: *Use simple and jargon-free language when possible.*

CHAPTER 9
MY BIG BUT

N ow it's time for my "big but." Some of my characterizations of the status and corporate executive perceptions of sustainability are pessimistic. *BUT* there are areas of significant progress and reasons for optimism, such as:

- Climate change is now recognized by numerous companies across industry sectors as a business risk, even in spite of the US political climate (pun intended). BlackRock, the world's largest asset manager with more than $6 trillion under management, is requiring 120 companies in its various portfolios to provide clear and specific climate risk disclosures. CEO Larry Fink's 2018 annual letter to CEOs states "a company's ability to manage environmental, social, and governance matters demonstrates the leadership and good governance that is so essential to sustainable growth, which is why we are increasingly integrating these issues into our investment process."[18] The CDP (formerly the

---

[18] While this appears meaningful, Andrew Winston pointed out in the Harvard Business Review that "[t]his is the fourth straight year that Fink's letter has made the pitch for long-term thinking and sustainability" and that the CEO audience may not actually be concerned with such a letter. Winston and others have noted that BlackRock runs index, or passive, funds, which

Carbon Disclosure Project, a UK-based non-profit that surveys companies globally about their greenhouse gas emissions and water use) reported progress in climate change and water use reporting in their network. ExxonMobil agreed to enhance its financial disclosures to include aspects of climate change.

- Energy technology continues to move forward, becoming mainstream and driving costs down to historic lows competitive with traditional fuel sources. The International Renewable Energy Agency (IRENA) estimates that pricing parity may be achieved as soon as 2020.

- Energy saving projects are popular because governmental incentives reduce a company's investment cost and have a well-defined and rapid ROI.

- Electric vehicles are now common and concerns perceived by consumers continue to be eliminated.

- Companies are evolving sustainability programs and reporting to be more pragmatic and less philosophical.

- ESG and impact investors are now common and growing in numbers and asset values. GoldmanSachs announced it has more than $10 billion in assets "tied to ESG investing activities" and established a new ETF focused on ESG.

- The amount of global investment value in green bonds sets a new record each year.

---

limits their effectiveness as an activist investor.

- Information technology is enabling unprecedented supply chain visibility and traceability.

- Product design with a higher level of recycling/reuse in mind has gained ground.

- Diversity, equality, and harassment at all levels within companies is a frequent topic of discussion, shareholder action and media coverage.

- Human rights, slavery and working conditions are recognized as elements of the global economy. Laws have been enacted in California and the UK requiring public disclosure of potential slavery in supply chains and the associated due diligence activities undertaken.

- Global water use/value is getting more attention than ever.

- The EU enacted its non-financial reporting directive requiring covering a range of matters, including sustainability.

A multitude of studies heralds the tipping point of real sustainability. Indeed, data show marked improvement in corporate uptake of sustainability matters/programs in the past five years. McKinsey & Co. reported that 70% of companies surveyed in 2017 have some form of sustainability/CSR governance in place compared with 56% in 2014, and 16% now have a Board committee for sustainability issues. KPMG's 2017 survey of corporate responsibility reporting covered the top 100 companies by revenue in 49 countries and the top 250 globally by revenue based on 2016 Fortune rankings. The study demonstrated impressive gains in sustainability matters and reporting in their sample. Large multinationals have significant economic, social and environmental impacts, and in many cases, are leaders in sustainability and social responsibility. Clearly, they have resources to apply to issues facing them, and they are some of the most recognizable brands on the planet. GoldmanSachs research showed that "larger companies do tend to score better on E&S metrics." Sustainability/CSR successes by big companies blazed the trails for others, although not every organization has chosen to go down the trail.

Niche companies have been founded on sustainability and/or social responsibility offerings. Organic foods, plant-based meat analogues, alternative cleaning chemicals, shoes, eyeglasses, textiles/clothing, restaurants, and transportation are but a few examples of industries with successful products based on a sustainability/social responsibility key element or offering.

This trend of sustainability successes is a reason to be cheerful, but a treasure trove of unidentified opportunities exists in other organizations. A 2016 compilation and analysis of US Census and IRS data indicates that small companies dominate the 5.7 million US enterprises with B2B relationships. Of the small businesses, 99% have revenues of $1 billion or less.[19] In terms of employee numbers, 96% of the companies have fewer than 50 employees. These companies are not reflected in the sustainability studies and statistics above.

---

[19] Only 2,894 US B2B enterprises identified reported annual revenues exceeding $1 billion.

Key point: *Sustainability generally remains the domain of big companies and certain industries. Internal challenges to sustainability/CSR in smaller companies are frequently greater than in large companies.*

Resources and possibly market visibility are more limited, and internal competition for funding and attention is higher than in larger companies. There is also the awkward truth that small companies may not always be as sophisticated or forward-thinking as big corporations. With all that, progress in sustainability/CSR has been slower, and more work may be required to convince management in smaller organizations. As discussed earlier, sources of pragmatic information/guidance for smaller companies are hard to come by and are not inexpensive.

Sustainability/CSR practitioners need to find new ways of approaching and discussing the topic within their organizations and convince others that dedicating resources will return business value.

CHAPTER 10
FIVE GUYS, TWO CENTS

In order to move beyond old, tired and uninspiring conversations about sustainability/CSR, we need to expand our view of what is relevant. In this regard, economists have been useful to sustainability professionals in the past, and still are. Today, however, we need to look to neuroscience, linguistics and behavioral science not usually considered part of the corporate sustainability context.

In that light, let's get our two cents' worth out of five guys: Milton Friedman, George Lakoff, Richard Thaler, Per Espen Stoknes and William Nordhaus.

Milton Friedman

The winner of the 1976 Nobel Prize for Economics, Friedman is often pilloried by sustainability professionals. He was a staunch supporter of free markets and did much work in price theory - the idea that markets determine the pricing of goods/services and serve economic needs of governments. A video series of fifteen lectures made at US universities from 1977 - 1989 called *Milton Friedman Speaks,* available on the Internet, is a great resource for anyone interested in learning more about his theories.

Friedman raises the hackles of sustainability professionals because of his essay "The Social Responsibility of Business is to Increase its Profits," published in the *New York Times* September 13, 1970. In the essay, Friedman argued that businesses' sole purpose is to generate profit for shareholders. He equated social responsibility with "pure and unadulterated socialism," and attacked "discussions of social responsibilities of business ... for their analytical looseness and lack of rigor." Moreover, he maintained companies that did adopt "responsible" attitudes would be faced with more binding constraints and therefore be less competitive than profit-focused companies.

At first glance, Friedman appears to destroy the very foundation of corporate sustainability. Lev, who was a colleague of Friedman's, softens the hard line somewhat by saying that Friedman would approve of sustainability/CSR investments where an opportunity arises that is within a company's core business competency, because it concurrently creates an appropriate profit opportunity. In *Winning Over Investors*, Lev offers several examples of companies that made CSR investments aligned with the business' capabilities. He also explained one not appropriately aligned: an American Express initiative that funded travel and tourism academies.

> *"....American Express's specialized capabilities in training such personnel [are not] obvious. True, the company has widespread travel operations, but its core business is finance and credit cards, not training."*

*Key point: Countering Friedman's position
on sustainability involves developing a
sustainable product that is clearly aligned with
the company's traditional offerings.*

Friedman also pointed out that "'business' as a whole cannot be said to have responsibilities." An interesting psychological foundation for this idea is explored later. This is not to say that companies are free to ignore legal boundaries in their pursuit of profits. Civins stated:

> *"Corporations are subject to laws that arguably deal with 'right and wrong,' e.g., Sarbanes Oxley, but whether they are or should be subject to ethical codes is not clear. There is the potential for legal exposure if a company's social and environmental programs undercut its ability to profitably conduct its core business or are inconsistent with shareholders' reasonable expectations, based on prior representations."*

Paradoxically, Friedman's emphasis that "only people can have responsibilities," brought clarity to a critical issue: human beings run companies, and those humans have their own individual morals and responsibilities, some of which may be considered social responsibilities. This is a critical and under-appreciated insight.

*Key point: Rather than attacking a "company,"
consumers and investors should try to influence corporate
managers by appealing to their personal sense of morals
and responsibilities.*

The remainder of this chapter explores how to convince individuals of the relevance of sustainability in a way that ironically proves Friedman (and by extension, many executives) wrong about corporate social responsibility.[20]

George Lakoff

Lakoff is a world-renowned linguist and cognitive scientist. His book *The All New Don't Think of an Elephant!* (2014) is a New York Times bestseller on framing public discourse. What Lakoff offers sustainability/CSR professionals is insight into the neuroscience and psychology of words, communication and framing debates.

Earlier, I summarized the development of environmental regulations creating an anti-regulatory mindset in business leaders. Lakoff explains even further that in 1970, well-funded political conservatives quietly implemented a policy to "ensure the best and brightest young people did not become anti-business." Conservatives funded institutes and endowed professorships to teach pro-business values across the nation.[21] New research in neuroscience shows long-term repetition of a consistent message changes neural pathways – a physical change in the brain reprogramming that message as the brain's default circuitry. Stanley Kubrick apparently used real science in *A Clockwork Orange*'s portrayal of reprogramming Malcolm MacDowell's character, Alex. Today's

---

[20] Lev said in a recent interview that Friedman "liked to introduce a subject and then generate great debate on his suggestions, which he felt people could accept or reject. That, I think, is the case with his famous commentary on CSR."

[21] The Center for Public Integrity claims this is still happening relative to climate change science and policy development, although the focus is on judicial officials rather than industry leaders.

executives are often only one generation removed from those who were at university in the 1970s, and are likely to have the same anti-regulatory brain circuitry as those who were their mentors.

Key point: Established thinking is difficult to alter because physical neural pathways in the brain are not easily changed.

Hard-wired perceptions and interpretations in our brain create frames of ideas, thoughts, and information. Frames are the reference point against which the human brain processes information and makes decisions. They are part of our subconscious and work even when we don't realize it or want them to. When facts/information don't match existing hard wiring, facts are ignored so we can continue with the desired behavior. Getting frames to change requires time and continuous effort. Lakoff explained, "If the facts don't fit the frames in your brain, the frames in brain stay and the facts are ignored or challenged or belittled."

Altering frames is challenging in other ways. "When we negate a frame, we evoke the frame," says Lakoff, using the title of his book as an example. In attempting to comply with his command "don't think of an elephant," the brain unconsciously calls up an image of an elephant even when consciously trying to avoid doing exactly that. This is the psychological equivalent to Heisenberg's Uncertainty Principle in quantum mechanics - simply measuring subatomic particles influences their properties - and similar to Thaler's mere-measurement nudge discussed below.

Key point: When discussing sustainability/CSR, we may unintentionally evoke frames that undermine our ability to convince others of our position.

Lakoff states "when you argue against someone on the other side using their language and their frames, you are activating their frames ... undermining your own views." Again, consider the command "don't think of an elephant." If you push back, preferring to think about peacocks instead, elephant imagery is already in your conscious mind. Combat this by controlling the conversation using frames, words, and imagery aligned with *your position*, rather than defensively responding by acknowledging the other side's position, even in repudiation.

Richard Thaler

Thaler won the 2017 Nobel Prize in Economics for his work in establishing behavioral economics. His books, *The Winner's Curse: Paradoxes and Anomalies of Economic Life* (1992), *Nudge: Improving Decisions About Health, Wealth and Happiness* (2008), and *Misbehaving* (2015) are widely known.

Early in Thaler's career, he continually found anomalies in his research and wanted to understand them. He ended up uncovering a flaw in the foundation of economic theory going back to Adam Smith. Behavioral economics explains many deviations of real-world results from traditional models and expectations, and is a radical departure from historical economic thinking.

Traditional economic models are based on assumptions that people make perfect decisions.

Thaler refers to these fantasy beings as "Econs." Econs are Google in human form, immediately accessing every publicly available fact written about a product or investment. Econs mentally process information according to strict methodologies in microseconds. To an Econ, there is no such thing as preference - there is only right and wrong. Friedman's models are based on Econs, which is one reason he did not anticipate consumer *preferences* for ethical or green products - he only foresaw increases in corporate expenditures associated with social responsibility. Econs likewise see only increased costs; their decisions are made based solely on what is correct, rational.

Some current sustainability solutions require consumers to be "eco-Econs" - requiring significant mental effort and data that is not available. For instance, is it better to choose paper towels made from recycled fiber over an electric hand dryer that uses electricity from fossil fuels? It is a complicated question to which an Econ would already know the answer. A Human needs time to process limited and likely incomplete or biased information, and then make a decision based on personal experiences, preconceptions and time constraints applicable to that moment. Or one that is completely irrational.

Humans, from an economist's perspective, *misbehave.* Our decisions are sometimes not rational. Yet, those decisions are the fuel of economic engines. "It is easier to make money catering to people's foibles than it is in educating them," Thaler has said. That is important guidance for how sustainability professionals should approach executives. Words, therefore, can be used shrewdly and subtly to influence economic decisions/outcomes. This is framing, which was examined above.

Key point: Behavior is frequently driven by the wording in instructions, guidance or even naming products/services, whether intentional or not.

In his book *Nudge*, Thaler delved deeply into the human psychology of making choices based on external influences. Research has shown that humans are easily manipulated (intentionally or otherwise) by other humans. Brain imaging studies suggest that those being manipulated actually sense/interpret the situation in the same way as those doing the manipulating (more on this later).

Thaler describes choice architecture - the design of thoughtfully presenting information choices or options "in a way that will make choosers better off, as judged by themselves." Wording of options and the way they are offered impacts how people act and this behavior can be predicted. Choice architects influence behavior by how they offer information and choices. This is what Thaler calls a "nudge." Choice architecture and nudging principles include minimizing and focusing options, using careful wording to subtly influence behavior, and formatting the presentation of options. Fundamentally, choice architecture is about reducing cognitive effort and overload; making it easy to choose the "right" choice.

Key point: When presenting options for consumers or executives, apply choice architecture to reduce - or maximize - desired bias and behavior in the outcome. In other words, nudge.

Public disclosures may be a nudge. Toby Whitney, a staffer in former Congressman Jim McDermott's office, who worked on Section 1502 of the Dodd-Frank Wall Street Reform and Consumer Protection Act of 2010, cites an example. Section 1502 requires that publicly-traded companies disclose certain information to the US Securities and Exchange Commission about tin, tantalum, tungsten, and gold (called "3TG") in manufactured products. The law requires nothing more than disclosing if minerals/metals purchased come from the Democratic Republic of Congo (DRC) or its nine bordering countries. Congress enacted the provision to nudge changes in corporate procurement practices as a way to help prevent funding of paramilitary groups across Central Africa responsible for human rights abuses. While the governmental mandate has been widely criticized as costly overregulation, the nudge was successful in changing corporate behavior.[22]

Thaler himself supports the idea of mandated disclosure to spur market mechanisms for improving environmental, health and safety issues. He offers up the Emergency Planning and Community Right-to-Know Act of 1986 (EPCRA) in the United States as a success story. EPCRA consists of a number of required public disclosures about chemicals used at manufacturing facilities. One disclosure is the Toxic Release Inventory (TRI), which is an annual report of chemical releases from US manufacturing sites. The

---

[22] One may question whether a legal requirement is a nudge. In this case, the law only required disclosure. Any behaviors or actions taken as a result of what was disclosed is the nudge, as in Thaler's EPCRA example. This is different from legal obligations concerning sustainability/CSR requirements in supplier contract terms. A nudge applies to valid choices; selecting between legal compliance and noncompliance is not really a choice. Contract terms are more like a shove in the back.

TRI data is publicly available, creating a social nudge in the form of "environmental blacklists" published in media and by environmental groups. Companies are motivated to reduce releases and avoid being on any list. EPCRA did not mandate reductions or chemical substitutes, yet that is how companies responded in part.

Key point: Public disclosure can be an effective nudge for initiating change because executives wish to avoid being called out as a result of what is disclosed.

Prior to *Misbehaving*, a group of professors of marketing at William & Mary, Ohio State University and The University of Texas at Austin published "The Sustainability Liability: Potential Negative Effects of Ethicality on Product Preference." The group found evidence of negative consumer perceptions of certain products labeled with ethical attributes such as "sustainable" or "environmentally friendly." Their hypothesis was that "ethicality is positively associated with some types of benefits and negatively associated with other types of benefits."

Briefly, the authors demonstrated that customers frequently feel that improved ethical aspects of a product reduces the product's ability to fully perform its expected function, or "strength." The authors found that emphasizing a sustainability attribute caused customers to feel that strength was compromised. Examples used in the study include detergents, hand sanitizers, and tires.

In addition, the study demonstrated that consumers change behavior when they are being observed (such as in a survey scenario). Other research discussed in *Nudge* confirms, "people become more likely to conform when they know that other people will see what they have to say." If customers know they are being observed in a survey scenario, they tend to act in the "right" way in choosing between an obviously sustainable option and one that is neither obvious nor sustainable. Therefore, even the process of testing consumer preferences injects bias into results: "the mere-measurement effect is a nudge" according to Thaler. Past surveys about consumer willingness to pay more for certain environmentally-preferable product attributes have proven inaccurate when compared to actual purchasing behavior.

Key point: Consumers may not follow through on behaviors they demonstrate in market surveys or testing, so new products or marketing campaigns can be built on false expectations.

I once discussed this with a well-known consumer brand that was considering launching a national advertising campaign based on a very real sustainability attribute. The company felt that the risk of "sustainability liability" was high, and chose to pursue another strategy.

Per Espen Stoknes

Per Espen Stoknes is a Norwegian psychologist, economist, entrepreneur, author, professor, and a new member of Norwegian Parliament. Among his areas of expertise are climate and environmental strategies, behavioral economics, and economic psychology. Stoknes' 2015 book *What We Think About When We Try Not to Think About Global Warming: Toward a New Psychology of Climate Action* explains the why and what of human psychology behind behaviors, using climate change as the backdrop.

We have established that people respond to an issue or choice based on their frames. The manner in which something is framed can be intentional or unintentional. Sustainability can take advantage of this quirk in human behavior, or be its victim. Simply discussing risk reduction or loss prevention in a conversation automatically brings to mind negative frames of risk and loss.

Stoknes points out that humans hate financial losses about two times more than they like financial gains. The pain of losing one dollar has twice the psychological effect of the joy of earning that same dollar. Put another way, humans prefer avoiding risk more than we enjoy winning. Econs, of course, recognize that one dollar has the same absolute value regardless of whether it is gained or lost.

Key point: *Presenting a sustainability/CSR opportunity in terms of avoiding a risk/negative may be valuable because humans are psychologically biased to avoid risk, but it may be better to frame the opportunity in positive terms. Assess the best direction for a specific audience.*

Tempting as it may be to use the criminal conviction of a VW executive for his role in the automaker's emissions cover-up as an example of sustainability risk - think twice. Any conversation in the context of jail time may have unintended consequences. Stoknes presents a number of positive frames that can be applied to sustainability/CSR initiatives:

- **Preparedness.** Uncertainty about whether an event *may happen* shifts the frame from reality, so put the matter in the context of *how the company would respond* to a particular event. Consider the idea of insurance, which offers financial protection when the event does occur. Be careful to avoid inadvertently bringing risk into the conversation.[23]

- **Ethics**. This is a far more powerful frame today than it was in the past. Ethics is a "now" issue, so using it as a frame for sustainability/CSR conversations can be a winning strategy. But don't stretch too far – be reasonable.

- **Opportunity**. This seems the default starting point for corporate sustainability discussions: finding economic growth and value, new products/services, and underserved markets. Stoknes states "what we choose to purchase depends not only on price and technical information, but even more on how the choice is presented." Retailers have known this for years: product placement and shelf space are carefully designed for the intended presentation.

- **Move from a regulatory frame to a market-driven frame**. It may be challenging to find these in the sustainability/CSR context. For instance, in some areas, air emissions can be monetized. Recycling shifts a regulated waste to a raw material with market value. Where this is possible, there is probably new cash flow to highlight.

---

[23] Lev uses the insurance analogy as well and is a proponent of overtly putting sustainability/CSR in risk management terms. It is unclear if he considered the human behavioral response to doing so.

Cognitive dissonance is another part of human behavior that sustainability practitioners can leverage. Conflicting feelings, thoughts and behaviors experienced at the same time create internal tensions. When someone enjoys eating steak, but recognizes the environmental impact of commercial beef operations, there may be a twang of guilt when grilling that New York Strip. This is cognitive dissonance. A person can resolve the tension by changing behavior in response to their feelings or they may do the opposite.

Key point: To resolve the tension of cognitive dissonance, people can choose to change feelings or thoughts and continue their desired behavior.

Online retail appeals to society's demand for convenience. Transactions are reduced to a few clicks, effectively eliminating effort-based obstacles to leaving home, searching for products, waiting in lines and making purchases. Free shipping means convenience comes without added cost. Free shipping also means more shipping, which means more fuel is combusted for transporting the extra packages. Are people willing to sacrifice convenience (changing behavior) to align with their feelings about greenhouse gas emissions? Looking at the astounding success of Amazon and the growth of other on-line shopping venues, the answer is a resounding "No."[24]

---

[24] Looking only at on-line subscription box services for home delivery of food, beauty and other items, website visits grew 3000% between 2013 and 2016, and as of March 2016, there were 2000 on-line subscription box services, according to *Inc. Magazine*. Those numbers don't include newer market entrants. There are even gasoline delivery apps/services that burn fuel to deliver fuel to personal vehicles at prearranged times and locations, such as homes – eliminating the need for drivers to stop and refuel at a gas station.

Key point: *Once thoughts or feelings are altered to justify existing behavior, confirmation bias becomes another obstacle.*

Humans seek out information that confirms what we already think or feel. Executives hesitant to support sustainability will point to stories of failures and fall back on outdated corporate lore that sustainability does not create value. Even executive bias toward the sustainability professional personally can work for or against perception of the information by that executive.

A typical response is to continually present the facts over and over again, yelling them louder and louder "delug[ing] the listeners or readers with ever more facts, statistics, figures and ominous projections." But facts and information are perceived independently of the quality of underlying science.[25] Part of this perception involves "psychological distance in time, space, and locus of control," says Stoknes. The further the time horizon or the less direct the control, the stronger short-term thinking and motivations typical of C-suites become. Facts alone about long-term benefits of sustainability aren't likely to convince executives. And repeated repetition of facts will not change that.

Key point: *Framing sustainability appropriately to executives is a prerequisite to communicating facts and nudging toward the desired outcome.*

---

[25] This is exactly the chasm in the climate change debate between "climate deniers" and those convinced of the validity of climate change science.

William Nordhaus

Back to more traditional economic studies. Yale Economics Professor, William Nordhaus, authored a Working Paper in 2004 for the National Bureau of Economic Research (NBER) that dusted off a 50-year-old economic model on financial benefits of innovation. In the 1960s, German economist Joseph Schumpeter created a model for profits resulting from innovation, known as Schumpeterian profits. Nordhaus revisited Schumpeterian profits in his Working Paper.

According to Schumpeter, innovation can create "extra-normal profits" – profits higher than the normal expected ROI based on the investment risk. These extra-normal profits are short-lived and disappear once the innovation has been adopted by competitors, leveling the playing field. The term "first mover advantage" is frequently used to describe this phenomenon in a more general and intangible way.

Innovation can lead to lower production costs without a reduction in the price customers pay for the product, meaning increased profit for the innovator until such time as others "appropriate" the innovation and create more or less equal competition. New or unique products also come out of innovation. Drug companies vigorously defend patents on new drugs as long as they can. During the patent period, the patent holder essentially has a monopoly on the drug and its price. When the patent expires, generic versions of the drug become available at lower prices. The original patent holder experiences a triple-whammy due to the competition – revenue, profit margin and customer base all shrink. Bloomberg News recently reported on strategies used by pharmaceutical companies to "extend the exclusivity period of their wares" in order to maintain profit margins for as long as possible.

The longer a company holds its innovation on an exclusive basis, the longer those higher profits tend to be maintained. Nordhaus presents a formula for calculating values for the short-term extra-normal profits. Looking at historical data from 1948 – 2001, he estimated the Schumpeterian profits (i.e., the extra-normal profits only) to range from -1.3% (during the major recession of the 1970s) to a high of 6.3% of total corporate profits.

When asked if he considered the applicability to sustainability, Nordhaus responded that in the case of sustainability innovations, extra normal profits consist of two components - the social value gained and the hard dollar additional profits. While that may be technically true, putting a number to social value (also called externalities) is theoretical which runs counter to the intent of this book and therefore will be gleefully ignored here.

As pointed out above, Friedman's position on corporate responsibility equates it solely to social value, calling it "pure and unadulterated socialism." He did not foresee Schumpeterian profits from sustainability improvements, most likely because, in the 1970s, there were no such examples.

In 2015, Xie Fan of the School of Economics & Management at South China Normal University followed up on Nordhaus with a study more specific to sustainability matters. Fan explored whether innovations related to CO_2 emissions regulations in China had an economic development benefit, as well as an environmental one. Fan's summary states that

> *"...first of all, the environmental regulation affects the total factor productivity growth in China's pollution-intensive industries; in the second place, the environmental regulation does not promote producer's scientific and technological innovation level in China's pollution-intensive industries; in the third place, the environmental regulation has reduced Schumpeter profits in China's pollution-intensive industries."*

In findings complementary to Nordhaus and Fan, UC Davis Graduate School of Management professor Paul Griffin found that shareholder value suffered in response to voluntary public disclosures on conflict minerals. His research team

> *"...examined 206 companies from December 2010 through March 2012 and found those companies — half who had voluntarily disclosed before the law became mandatory — lost $6.5 billion in shareholder value due to declining equity values. Both disclosing and non-disclosing companies were affected because of the ripple effect in capital markets when uncertainties arise about a particular business practice — using conflict minerals, in this case."*

The study methodology claims to correct for other factors possibly influencing stock pricing before and after such disclosures. It is worth pointing out that Griffin found voluntary reporting induced a change in capital markets. While this is different from the company-specific profit picture painted by Nordhaus and Schumpeter, Griffin's results offer additional support for reconsidering the nature and scope of voluntary reporting.

In the end, both Fan and Nordhaus offer complementary models for sustainability value. Fan's point is that once an environmental issue becomes *regulated*, compliance innovation may no longer provide Schumpeterian profits, although this may contradict the Porter Hypothesis. Yet applying Nordhaus to *discretionary* sustainability business innovation, short-term extra-normal profits are to be expected and can be estimated. Griffin's findings indicate voluntary reporting on sustainability/CSR may have negative consequences in the valuation of equities.

Key point: *Maximizing short-term extra-normal profits resulting from sustainability innovations may involve reducing transparency in order to maintain the exclusivity of those innovations.*[26]

* * *

One final point about the nexus of behavioral economics and sustainability. Driving (and predicting) desired behaviors depends a great deal on cultural norms, which differ by region/culture. Something considered "sustainable" or "responsible" in the US may not be so in other countries.[27] Low laborer wages

---

[26] Lev argues that with the prevalence of corporate valuation now based on intangibles, the more and sooner investors have visibility into innovations (which tend to be in intangible assets in today's world), the higher they value the company, which is in contrast to Griffin. On the other hand, in 2017, Lev published *Evaluating Sustainable Competitive Advantage*, in which he said competitive advantage is achieved and maintained by the successful deployment of strategic assets, meaning those that are valuable, rare and difficult to imitate. Disclosing information on product innovation may be counter to ensuring that strategic assets indeed remain rare and non-imitable.

[27] New research that demonstrates this in the context of ESG investments is

in Asia and the use of child labor in developing countries are common but unacceptable to US sensibilities. The ugly truth is that in some cases, those individuals face worse choices; requirements forced onto others by US customers may have an unintended effect of pushing people toward a worse situation.

The current trend of supply chain sustainability initiatives may impose US cultural expectations against a headwind of centuries of local culture where supplier/contract manufacturers operate. This should be a consideration when seeking to change behaviors or expectations through a company's supply chain. US consumers are proving they lack an understanding of non-US cultural norms, meaning consumer products companies are squeezed by customer pressures to enforce supplier changes at one end, and by pushback on the other end from suppliers to allow them to operate without extra-territorial mandates. The ultimate benefits would improve the lives of millions across the globe, but some see only American imperialism and in Africa it has even been termed the "White Savior Complex."

---

discussed later.

CHAPTER 11
PAINFUL, PERSONAL AND UNSPOKEN

We have covered several realities of executive preconceptions, but one aspect of management's assessment of sustainability/CSR not yet discussed is insidious.

> **Key point:** *The internal perception of sustainability's place in the org chart, its leader and staff can predetermine a program's success or failure.*

A 2016 Bain & Company study on organizational aspects of sustainability indicated that only two percent of 300 companies surveyed actually achieved or exceeded the sustainability goals those companies established for themselves. Furthermore, a full 81% settled for what Bain called "dilution of value and mediocre performance" in sustainability. The reasons for this failure boil down to two themes: ineffective sustainability leadership and lack of convincing valuation of sustainability programs/efforts.

Although this perception is tremendously important, it is generally subtle and almost hidden from view. Of course, this happens elsewhere in organizations too -

"special projects departments" are famous holding areas in advance of retirement, forced and otherwise. Sustainability professionals must be prepared for a certain amount of internal negativity based solely on the perception by others in the organization.

Where?

Where sustainability/CSR resides in a company's organization speaks to how management values the function. It can be a stand-alone department or under another corporate function. McKinsey & Co. found that a gap exists between the reasons a company chooses to implement a sustainability/CSR initiative "and where in the company sustainability actions are pursued." Organizational placement varies by company - sustainability/CSR can be a part of:

- Marketing/Communications
- Environmental, Health and Safety
- Human Resources
- Operations
- Finance
- Executive office/Strategic Planning
- Compliance/Ethics/Legal
- Procurement/Sourcing/Trade
- Government Affairs/Public Affairs
- Investor Relations

By definition, a hierarchy has a top, middle, and a bottom. Each company has its own hierarchy of organizational importance and internal perception. Executive preconceptions burned in neural pathways related to corporate structure automatically create bias to either help or hinder sustainability/CSR. Sustainability program leaders may not be aware of what the biases are, which executives hold what bias, or which way the scales are tipped. They must figure out for themselves which rung of the ladder they sit on.

Key point: If the program is seen as an important part of the company, the pressure is on to retain that respect. Otherwise, time must be spent reframing and building credibility before perception changes.

Companies that emphasize the reporting element over program implementation usually place sustainability/CSR in the Marketing/Communications department. In these cases, sustainability is normally not considered an important strategic function. Being detached from Operations, these situations risk missing potentially valuable opportunities and lack credibility. The same can be said of Human Resources, Investor Relations, and even Government Affairs. I know one instance where the Marketing department leading a company's sustainability program decided to focus on their minimal use of one chemical, ignoring more significant aspects like packaging, plastic use and product transportation. Administrative groups tend to have minimal influence in Operations, product development or business strategy.

Moving up the ladder is Compliance/Ethics/Legal, but that can carry a negative connotation from which sustainability/CSR may not easily detach. Environmental, Health and Safety is another step in the right direction because of ongoing interaction with Operations, management, and procurement.

Procurement/sourcing/trade is next since that tends to be the epicenter of supplier and raw material controls.

The top rung of organizational credibility for sustainability/CSR is Operations, Finance or Executive Office/Strategic Planning, depending on the company culture. With Operations at the helm, a sustainability program becomes directly embedded in the manufacturing culture, albeit not immediately. When Finance is responsible for sustainability, the emphasis is on valuation using the organization's applicable financial metrics that carry credibility and influence with Operations and the C-suite. And of course, if the C-suite takes a specific interest in sustainability/CSR, then it tends to happen. Looking back at articles about sustainability/CSR success at major brands, the C-suite is featured on a regular basis.

Bain & Company offered realistic perspectives on the topic:

> *"Often, enthusiastic leadership teams overlook the difficulties frontline employees confront when implementing new approaches. If employees feel forced to choose between sustainability targets and business targets, for example, most choose business targets... In our survey, 62% of respondents cited public reputation as the primary business rationale for sustainability programs - nice to have, but not essential to the business."*

Where sustainability/CSR sits in the company structure goes a long way to projecting the image of whether the function is nice to have or essential. Every company has its own character, organization, leadership style and culture, so these observations may not fit into a particular organization. As an aside, anyone seeking a new position in a corporate sustainability/CSR program should consider this as well.

Who? (He's on First)

Every corporate function, regardless of where it fits in the organization, is a reflection of its leader. Personality, technical skills, business acumen, interpersonal skills and communication all factor into how a leader is perceived by others and the judgments made about the leader. The Bain study pointed out that sustainability leaders must "affirm that the benefits of creating a sense of commitment significantly outweigh the risks."

What characteristics and in what mix are most important for someone leading a sustainability program? It depends on the specific organization, including the "Where" of the sustainability program.

Key point: Finding the right leader involves clearly defining what sustainability/CSR means to the company, evaluating candidates against criteria based on that definition and determining if/how gaps can be closed.

Position needs and requirements for success must be clearly defined and prioritized. That shouldn't be anything new. The trick, however, is how candidates are assessed against them. Some gaps may be easily bridged through training or education; others are personality traits core to an individual's character. Where a candidate demonstrates a large gap in a core trait, the organization faces a choice: either move on to another candidate, or be fully aware that old neural pathways need to be altered for new behaviors and ways of thinking to take hold. It is unlikely typical training/awareness programs will close these types of gaps. Significant investment in that individual will not necessarily guarantee success. The Leadership Wheel© originally developed by Commander Kerry F. Gentry, USN (Ret.) helps visualize these concepts (Figure 1).

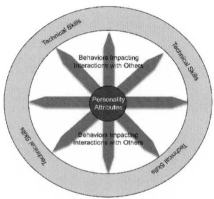

Figure 1: The Leadership Wheel ©

The hub provides the stable structural center of a bicycle wheel. In a leadership context, fixed core personality traits form the hub. Behaviors (the spokes) rely on and extend out of the core traits (hub). Technical skills, like tires, are the easiest of the elements to change. Spokes (behaviors) can be tuned and maintained. Hub bearings are replaced – rather than repaired - when they are the source of a wheel problem. When the hub is not centered correctly, the entire wheel wobbles no matter how strong the other parts are. When assessing sustainability/CSR leadership, seek out a strong hub aligned with the company, spokes that are appropriate and tuned, and a tire strong enough to get the work done. There is no sense in hiring a wobbly wheel, but it may make sense to patch up a weak tire on a good wheel.

A similar situation is safety. At a plant level, safety leadership requires influencing behaviors of a wide range of people. Changing a long-embedded operating culture of "production first" is challenging. If the safety leader's abilities do not extend beyond technical safety expertise, his/her impact will be noticeably limited. I have seen this happen at many manufacturing sites. To be effective, a leader requires proficiency in interpersonal skills and cultural awareness at a minimum. The goal is to change long-established mindsets and behaviors of people whose priorities typically center on production. Convincing folks to rearrange their existing priorities means making them think safe behaviors are their idea. A leader sets guideposts for desired behavior and nudges others to believe it is their own idea to stay within those guideposts.

What? (Second base!)

What qualifications are necessary for a sustainability/CSR program leader? There is no right answer to this question, especially since sustainability is inherently cross-functional. But executives, especially those with an operations background, tend to be leery of sustainability/CSR professionals without practical business or manufacturing experience. They harbor concerns that initiatives will be unrealistic and may even embarrass them in front of peers. A program leader with a primarily "soft" background like policy or

NGO experience may have a harder time establishing internal credibility than someone with a business or technical background. It is also possible to be too far on the technical end; engineers who have spent their career designing bridges using mathematical precision may have difficulties dealing with uncertain, ambiguous and human elements of sustainability/CSR.

Key point: If your background is a concern, tackle that perception by continually reinforcing the present and future of sustainability/CSR initiatives in a credible manner.

Don't get wrapped up in conversations about your past. Sustainability is about what lies ahead, so maintain that perspective as much as possible. Be careful about referring to past experiences.

Sustainability leaders today have a range of degrees including philosophy, chemistry, biology, business, liberal arts, law and of course, engineering. Universities now offer sustainability degrees, including graduate programs. Business schools are integrating sustainability courses into their MBA curriculum. These are encouraging developments indeed, and offer a glimpse of the future of executive thinking. For now, however, old perceptions remain an obstacle.

CHAPTER 12
THE PLAGUE

A plague oftentimes infects corner offices. Not the Bubonic Plague but something just as contagious: "short-termism." This disease causes executives to focus almost exclusively on quarterly financial performance instead of establishing and managing toward long-term goals.[28] Over the years, academics, financial experts and consultants have published numerous studies, reports and analyses about the damage caused by short-termism.[29]

Short-termism is problematic in several ways but it squeezes off blood flow to sustainability/CSR, which by definition is a long-term view of the world. Without the flow of support and funding, sustainability/CSR becomes lifeless, ending in amputation. Where the C-suite seeks quick pops in stock price, studies show they eschew making investments that don't manifest in that way. According to studies reviewed by CFO Magazine, "[q]uarters when CEO equity awards vest coincide with

---

[28] Chris Ailman, Chief Investment Officer of CalSTRS with a portfolio of over US$200 billion, said "It bothers me that the average CEO considers the long term to be 91 days from now, when it should be about 30 years."

[29] A report by Network for Business Sustainability Canada, cited in the bibliography, contains an extensive literature list on short-termism and long-term thinking. In *The End of Accounting*, Lev said "the pressure of day-to-day operations often distracts managers from the long-term thinking required to institute protective mechanisms for strategic assets."

corporate actions that pump up stock prices briefly while damaging the company's long-term value."

Harvard Business School professor Ananth Raman put it succinctly:

> *"There are many reasons for managers not to ignore the short-term price. The obvious one is that they are often compensated with stock options, whose value is based on the firm's current stock price... Under pressure to manage the short-term stock price - and at times meet short-term earnings target - many managers told me that they had abandoned sound projects with good long-term value because these investments would not help, and could often hurt, their stock price."*

This plague also infects institutional investment managers that, in many cases, have their own short-term pay-for-performance incentives. These investment managers place additional pressure on corporate executives at the helm of companies that part of the investor portfolio.

There are long-term investors doing things differently. Vanguard CEO William McNabb penned "An open letter to directors of public companies worldwide" on August 31, 2017 emphasizing that their index funds are structurally long-term and pointing out the four pillars of governance Vanguard applies. In a panel discussion in late 2016, Ted Eliopoulos, Chief Investment Officer of CalPERS, with a portfolio of $300 billion said that "performance on sustainability goals is now part of our qualitative incentive performance review. Our internal managers are being

evaluated in part on the progress we've been making in
implementing the ESG strategic plan that we just
adopted." McKinsey's Koller states that:

> *"...we often find that executives themselves
> or their boards are usually the source of
> short-termism ... rather than investors,
> analysts and others outside the
> company..."*

ESG investors, discussed later, have a long-term
investment horizon intended to encourage companies
to invest in sustainability/CSR initiatives. ESG
investment strategies are gaining in popularity and
becoming mainstream, but are still in the minority
compared with those focused on quarterly results. Bain
found that companies that are successful at achieving
sustainability goals "change their capital-approvals
process to include sustainability factors, or increase
time horizons in business case assessments, allowing
more initiatives to qualify for investment."
GoldmanSachs similarly found that "E&S metrics work
better as a signal for long-term (rather than shorter-
term) stock price performance."

> ***Key point:*** *Executives have incentives to manage short-
> term financial performance that can compromise long-
> term thinking. In these situations, the credibility of the
> sustainability/CSR organization, leader and financial
> justification are crucial, as is the ability to effectively frame
> the value.*

Chapter 13
Kill Sustainability

Sustainability has value, and yet it is not widely valued. One could even say it is loathed in some executive suites. McKinsey & Co. reported that companies' "pursuit of growth-related activities has declined in recent years." In my experience, some of this comes simply from the word sustainability itself, not the concept or value it is intended to describe.[30] So, stop using the word "sustainability."

Sustainability professionsals will choke on this. Why *de-emphasize the very thing my job depends on?* As discussed earlier, management is likely focused on traditional drivers/metrics of the company's financial performance. Capital is limited, revenues need to increase, costs need to decrease, the stock price is too low and competitors are gaining market share. Cynical executives only need one reason to divert attention/funding. Remember the audience. Pride can't get in the way of success. Does it really matter if an initiative is called sustainability, cost optimization, strategy or flying pigs?

---

[30] Michelle Edkins, Managing Director at BlackRock and Global Head of its Investment Stewardship team, said this from her perspective as a major institutional investor: "You typically don't get much reaction from companies when you ask about ESG or sustainability."

Key point: *To many executives, the word sustainability is a cue to stop listening based on existing frames.*

Imagery entering their thinking includes:

- The lack of a consistent, reasonable and/or actionable definition to which they can relate, and use of incomprehensible jargon.

- Bias of the executives against change or the options offered.

- Expectations of inappropriate, unrealistic or inconclusive value.

- Fear of choices that are new or unfamiliar.

- Perceptions of product performance tradeoffs.

- Inconsistency with short term financial pressures.

- Perceptions about the sustainability function and staff.

Approaching internal decision makers in a way that recognizes their terms usually results in a higher likelihood of success (i.e., framing). Conversations do not need to be wholly on their terms, but it is necessary to understand what their terms are and if you can use them in some way. Sun Tzu in *The Art of War* said: "Every matter requires previous knowledge."

In *Nudge*, Thaler pointed out a situation sustainability/CSR practitioners fear:

> *"In most firms, managers do not think that being the guy who pushes an energy cost-saving policy is the route to the CEO office, especially when the cost savings are small relative to the bottom line. The project sounds boring and penny-pinching,*

*and the manager who suggests it might be
destined for a job in accounting, rather
than the president's office."*[31]

This is one reason why sustainability professionals
are motivated to be unreasonably creative without
considering how doing so affects their credibility. We
use too much of the executives' own frames and force
our goals into them. Instead, take time to understand
the company, how it operates and build *your* frames
from there. Learn as much as possible, such as:

- What does the company make or offer? What
  need does it fill? Why does that need exist in
  the first place?

- What costs are built into product pricing?

- Why do customers buy from the company?
  What are customers' key buying criteria?

- What is important in a new product? How is
  the market analyzed and demand predicted?

- What are key internal words, phrases,
  programs and initiatives? Is the executive
  culture one that is willing to make tough
  business decisions when necessary?

- What are the manufacturing processes
  involved? What is the status of manufacturing
  capacity, efficiency or limitations?

- What are the most critical aspects of revenue
  generation and profitability? What are the

---

[31] To Thaler's point: Tim Balcon, CEO of the UK's Institute of Environmental
Management and Assessment wrote in 2015 that "40% of ISO 14001 users
saved at least £10,000 ... since implementation."   The standard was first
published in 1996; £10,000 in savings over what could be twenty-two years is
likely to irritate management due to the poor ROI of the initial investment and
ongoing costs to maintain the effort.

direct and indirect cost drivers with the biggest impact?

- Why are certain suppliers used? What are the company's key buying criteria?

- Who are the most important audiences for the company's external communications?

- Why do employees choose to work at the company? What is important to them? What are the different relevant compensation programs, metrics, and triggers?

- Is the company seeking to attract certain investor groups?

Key point: Building sustainability/CSR choice architecture that appropriately balances executive points of view and new sustainability frames requires effort and skill.

Identify where sustainability initiatives may make sense within the company's operating context. Where a potential project is identified, discuss *relevant* business benefits using the appropriate business words. Link initiatives to key buying criteria or other customer requirements. Focus on real economic value created and try to avoid couching value in terms of risk avoidance. Eliminate the unnecessary barrier, artificial distinction and separation from business that "sustainability" creates - don't use the word until near the end of any conversation: "Oh, and it's a sustainability success, too."[32] Michelle Edkins of BlackRock suggested using "language of long-term

---

[32] I published an article with that quote a few years ago and in a November 2, 2017 interview with Bloomberg News, Lloyd Blankfein, CEO of GoldmanSachs, used that line. I'd love to say he stole it from me, but that would be a lie.

operational excellence ... innovation and adaptation and sustainable financial performance, the companies tend to be very fluent and well-versed in those issues."

If we recognize that sustainability is nothing more than an emotionally charged synonym for business, operational efficiency or strategy, then the word and related tension it causes are completely unnecessary. Ironically, we circle back to Freidman's view that the responsibility of corporations is to generate profits. But in this case, profits from sustainability.

After doing groundwork about the company's specific situation, it can be worthwhile to link to developments, ideas, and methodologies that exist outside the company. Some are reasonable and worthwhile; others are more likely to be a wild goose chase. Or squirrel chase as I call it.

CHAPTER 14
SQUIRRELS

Dogs and sustainability/CSR professionals are easily distracted. Squirrels immediately capture canine attention, triggering a frantic chase. The squirrels of sustainability include new fads, reporting guidelines, fantastic claims of financial value, as well as customer requirements.

__Key point:__ Some sustainability squirrels are worth catching; others, perhaps not. Sustainability practitioners should critically evaluate each and make the determination.

There are many from which to choose. I've selected a mere handful (there are others not listed here) and assigned each a rating as follows:[33]

- three squirrels mean it is high value right now and should be given serious consideration. These may also be legal or customer requirements and therefore, not really discretionary.

---

[33] For instance, attracting and retaining talent, the UN Sustainable Development Goals and the EU Non-Financial Reporting Directive are excluded from this chapter. Their absence here does not reflect any specific intent; I simply chose to cover other topics. The SDGs and concerns in applying them at a company level are touched on earlier in the book.

- two squirrels mean it is worth looking into now and deciding how/if to move forward based on the assessment.

- one squirrel means the activity has questionable or no value at the moment. It could become important in later years, but it's a crapshoot. The prudent thing to do is sit back and monitor the situation for now.

Customers

The customer-supplier relationship is the basic element of the supply chain, and has already been explored. Few links in the chain succeed by ignoring their customers. Jeff Bezos, Amazon's CEO, once explained the company's success is because "we start with the customer and we work backward." The sustainability context is no different - understand customers' key buying criteria, how their perceptions of sustainability impact decisions and then meet their needs. I gave a presentation on this idea in 2002 to an association of corporate environmental leaders, but that was too far ahead of its time and the audience was not engaged. Today companies understand that customers have a variety of sustainability/CSR expectations and requirements, ranging from completing questionnaires, agreeing to being audited by third parties, to reducing product packaging or more.

Consumers are likely to present new opportunities to those whose products they buy. Companies should listen to complaints on sustainability/CSR matters – those are an unfiltered map for what customers seek, which may be an unmet need in the overall market. Tracking social media is an easy and essentially free way of finding this information in real time.

Business-to-business (B2B) relationships can be more difficult than business-to-consumer (B2C) relationships. The world's largest brick and mortar retailer is famous for the tough requirements it imposes on suppliers. So tough, in fact, that the retailer required that cost savings achieved by suppliers as a result of sustainability initiatives were to be reflected in price reductions for products sold to that retailer. Suppliers in this scenario won very little because they could not harvest the value of the initiatives - all value rested with that customer. In this case, there was little financial incentive for suppliers to undertake sustainability efforts since they were not a mandatory condition of the contract.

In the end, however, meeting customer desires isn't really discretionary, so this is a "must do," and again, high value. So go after this squirrel.

CDP

CDP, formerly the Carbon Disclosure Project, is a UK-based non-profit that has operated for 15 years. They claim "the most comprehensive collection of self-reported environmental data in the world." CDP is very well known and is essentially the standard for reporting greenhouse gas emissions. They also collect and track water use data. Completing a CDP questionnaire can be quite involved, time-consuming and frustrating. However, customers frequently require a completed questionnaire, so it is effectively a mandate. As such, I consider it high value, although it is limited to environmental aspects of sustainability.

Statement of Significant Audience and Materiality

Reporting frameworks, concepts, and philosophies abound, but they typically try to be all things to all users. The Global Reporting Initiative (GRI) has been around for two decades, but only recently issued what they call their first global standards for sustainability reporting encompassing economic, environmental and social impacts.[34] Covering too much ground in a report waters down the message and adds pages to no valid purpose. Not all sustainability information is important (or material) to all audiences. In partial response, attempts have been made to narrow information to what is material, although as discussed previously, that is itself fraught with ambiguity. There is no single "reasonable investor" to which sustainability/CSR materiality can be generally linked.

---

[34] In response to what GRI saw as a "service that fills a much-needed gap in the market," they launched a Disclosure Review Service in January 2018 covering "a selection of 10 disclosures ... focusing on the application of the GRI Materiality and Stakeholder Inclusiveness Principles."

In researching his latest book, Baruch Lev chose not to "presume to know what information investors need." Instead, he spent a year assessing what information is actually important to investors and in doing so:[35]

> *"...analyz[ed] hundreds of quarterly analyst (earnings) calls. Keep in mind that an analyst may have just one opportunity to ask the question. There were no — no — questions ever raised about ESG performance, corporate sustainability, and related topics. We reviewed, as I said, hundreds of earnings calls, with about 25-to-30 questions on each call."*

This is a powerful statement. Lev's extensive research proved that investors increasingly need sources other than financial reporting for information that is important to investment decisions (in other words, "material" information), which is reflected directly in stock prices. Yet in analyzing "hundreds of quarterly analyst calls" over multiple years, not one analyst raised a question about sustainability, CSR or ESG. Once again, the question about the importance or materiality of sustainability/CSR to mainstream investors is unresolved.

Robert G. Eccles and Tim Youmans of Harvard Business School offered an excellent solution to the reasonable investor conundrum. Eccles and Youmans propose that a company's Board of Directors identify and assess various relevant audiences for the company's sustainability/CSR disclosure, determine what audience(s) are most important to the company, and issue a Statement of Significant Audiences and Materiality that explicitly defines the audience for

---

[35] Recall that Lev chose to use the word "important" rather than "material."

whom the sustainability/CSR disclosure is primarily intended. That, in turn, clarifies the reference point for materiality in sustainability/CSR reporting. Former SEC Chairwoman Mary Shapiro commented in 2016 that in order for companies to "develop the most useful and cost-effective disclosure practices, investors themselves will have to become more active in communicating their own demands and preferences for information." If investors follow Shapiro's advice, Boards will have an easier time making Significant Audience determinations and Statements.

These Statements are not common, but they should be.

ESG Ratings and Investors

Environmental, social and governance (ESG) ratings and investments are new squirrels but not likely to be a mere fad.[36] ESG is essentially the terminology the investment community uses to mean sustainability/CSR. There are ESG investors, funds, screens and ratings - each with a different way of judging ESG value and impact on corporate performance. References included in the bibliography provide explanations and comparisons of a few of these.

---

[36] However, Chris Ailman of CalSTRS mentioned that "the word "sustainability" had a stigma for a while. Now 'ESG' apparently carries the same kind of stigma."

There is mounting evidence of the positive correlation between ESG performance and financial performance.[37] This relationship is not definitive, and uncertainty in the underlying data used in investment ratings raise some questions on its own about the reality. One large ESG rating firm, MSCI, published a paper that took a different path in assessing the correlation.

MSCI agrees that "correlation does not imply causation" when considering linkages between ESG performance and corporate financial performance. Instead of looking at whether or why there is correlation, they analyzed *how* ESG information creates "financially significant effects." To explain the *how*, MSCI identified three "transmission channels" for ESG information flow to investors. Two of the channels, named the "idiosyncratic risk channel" and the "valuation channel" are influenced directly by companies. The third (the "systemic risk channel") refers to market-wide events (e.g., interest rates, global market shocks, etc.); how an individual company fares in response to such events is known as beta, a numerical indicator of a stock's volatility in comparison to the overall market (expressed as a ratio), which relates back to valuation. [38]

Idiosyncratic risk is simply company-specific risk. MSCI claims that companies with good ESG

---

[37] A study by the University of Oxford (UK) and Arabesque Partners (2014) does an excellent job or summarizing much of the existing literature on ESG and investors, as well as providing a few of its own insightful conclusions. Anyone interested in the topic should read this report.

[38] *Investopedia* explains volatility this way: "a higher volatility means that a security's value can potentially be spread out over a larger range of values. This means that the price of the security can change dramatically over a short time period in either direction. A lower volatility means that a security's value does not fluctuate dramatically, but changes in value at a steady pace over a period of time."

performance are "better at managing company- specific and operational risks and therefore have a lower probability of suffering incidents that can impact their share price." ESG performance therefore is an indicator of overall business risk management, rather than being inherently and independently valuable. [39]

MSCI's valuation risk is more complicated, meaning my explanation gets into the weeds a bit. A prerequisite to understanding valuation risk is knowing a little about cost of capital (CoC). A company's CoC is not just the interest rate it pays on debt. Investors have expectations when they give companies their money in exchange for shares. These expectations are the returns they want on their investment and are a component of CoC. Attracting and keeping investors (i.e., capital) means making sure the company's use of capital generates returns that are adequate to meet investor expectations.[40] Higher returns are expected from companies seen as high risk, while investors accept lower returns from more stable investments.[41]

MSCI asserts that investors view companies with good ESG performance as having lower systemic risk and beta, therefore reducing the expected CoC. This, according to MSCI, results in "higher company valuations."[42,43]

---

[39] This is consistent with findings from a GoldmanSachs analysis that with "a selective suite of key ESG metrics, mainstream investors can add a differentiated and alpha-additive complement of risk analysis." While beta is presented as a ratio, Investopedia defines alpha as a specific stock's actual "return on an investment that is not a result of general movement in the greater market" – in other words, company-specific risk.

[40] This is what EVA®, discussed in a previous chapter, is intended to assess and what Koller describes as a foundation of corporate value.

[41] Put another way, investors expect higher returns from stocks with high beta, therefore higher beta means higher CoC.

[42] The study goes into great detail about the transmission channels and the study methodology. I recommend reading it.

[43] Thaler disputes that beta is meaningful. In *Misbehaving*, he said, "The *facts*

One final observation about CoC. A pair of finance professors at Germany's University of Aachen published new research highlighting two interesting points: first, almost all prior research into the ESG/CoC linkage has been limited to the US market; and second, the strength of the ESG/CoC linkage correlates closely to social culture. In countries with cultures that value social responsibility (such as the US), the authors claim that ESG improvements lowered CoC. However, in countries where social responsibility is not a part of the culture, the influence of ESG on CoC was weaker.[44] Countries with a lower culture score in the study included Singapore, Thailand and Nigeria.

Consistency and comparability are not hallmarks of ESG investment tools at this time. GoldmanSachs research found that "one widely used ESG database has expanded its number of available data points by nearly 5X since 2010 to over 6,000,000 today." Baruch Lev was recently quoted as saying "ESG metrics are not yet at investment-grade."

A report from Principles for Responsible Investment (PRI) assessing the level of attention paid to ESG by investment consultants stated that:

> *"...investment consultants provide little advice on implementing responsible investment, integrating ESG issues into*

---

are that the capital asset pricing model has clearly been rejected as an adequate description of the movements of stock prices. Beta, the only factor that was once thought to matter, does not appear to explain very much." Yet beta remains prevalent in investment evaluations. For instance, Koller uses beta in valuation methodologies presented in his book.

[44] This makes sense. Cultural values vary in countries with their own stock exchanges around the world. If exchanges generally appeal to "local" investors, the local cultural setting will influence investment decisions. The three countries with the weakest ESG/CoC correlation each have their own stock exchanges.

> *investment research and decision-making, or on monitoring the ESG performance of asset managers. Despite pockets of excellence and some high profile projects on issues such as climate change and long-term investment, ESG considerations are not a standard part of the advice offered by investment consultants. They are widely seen as niche service offerings, often entailing extra costs, and only to be provided when explicitly requested by asset owner clients."*

I was part of a panel on ESG data in late 2017. In the audience were representatives of ratings agencies and investors who almost universally expressed concern about the credibility of the data they receive from companies in response to their inquiries. In 2016, PricewaterhouseCoopers (PwC) similarly found that while 100% of companies who report ESG data are confident in the quality of that data, only 29% of investors share that sentiment. Edkins of BlackRock has said their analysts are "deeply skeptical about company-reported ESG data right now." A July 2017 article by a group of accounting and finance professors at Montclair State University concluded this after studying consistency across major ESG ratings:

> *"...little consistency exists across the ratings from the three agencies examined... The commonalities are so few that a statistically valid analysis comparing rankings and ratings cannot be performed... The underlying methodology used to identify,*

score, and rank each company varies, as do the KPIs used and the weighting percentages of categories."

Some ratings agencies and investors simply make do with what they consider to be unreliable data. Others do their own research and fulfill data needs in other ways, such as adding publicly available information in their algorithms. That sounds nice, but it adds inconsistency beyond just the various algorithms themselves.[45]   The initiatives/standards scope sustainability differently and the models are different - each a proprietary black box. At my panel discussion, there were suggestions of creating a raw ESG data set that was independently verified and not "processed," so each proprietary algorithm could use the information in its own way and reduce the questionnaire burden on companies. [46]

Organizations have differing opinions on ESG ratings and their importance. Make that assessment before chasing this squirrel.

---

[45] RobecoSAM's Corporate Sustainability Assessment Methodology, which "forms the research backbone" of the Dow Jones Sustainability Indices, claims to be "unique in that it is based on information provided by the companies through the online questionnaire.   This allows RobescoSAM to analyze sustainability at a much deeper level than frameworks based on public disclosure alone."

[46] A representative of one large company told me she completes more than 100 ESG questionnaires a year from customers, investors and ratings agencies. Her company is a service provider, not a manufacturer.

Sustainability/CSR Reporting

This squirrel can be a major distraction. Such a statement is considered heresy and treason to a large group of sustainability/CSR practitioners because of the historical emphasis on and perceived importance of reporting. Sustainability programs should focus on implementation, not on the report. A company can have an excellent sustainability program without reporting on it or may reflect it poorly in a report. Supporters will argue that the process of developing a sustainability/CSR report aligned with an internationally recognized framework, in and of itself, drives companies to develop programs and execute them. To some extent, that is true.

What tends to be more common is the opposite - a company publishes a beautiful sustainability report aligned with a reporting framework, but the actual program maturity and implementation differ meaningfully from what is communicated in the report. Sustainability reports are reviewed by many corporate departments, and are carefully worded works of art. What is omitted or implied can be more telling than what is actually on the pages. Lev recently commented that "the 'how-wonderful-we-are' communications by large public companies are not really relevant to investors."

The 2017 KPMG sustainability/CSR reporting survey found that the two sectors with the lowest level of reporting are Industrials, Manufacturing and Metals (industries in which my experience is concentrated) and retail. The inclusion of retail in this list is baffling given the activity and money spent on CSR programs by that sector.

Sustainability/CSR reporting is not without some legal risk as well. According to Civins (the Texas environmental attorney mentioned earlier):

> *"To the extent a company falls short of written public commitments, including commitments regarding suppliers, there is the potential for regulatory and private litigation based on, among other things, fraudulent statements involving securities."*

Indeed, in the 1990s, Nike was sued for public statements it made about working conditions in factories that manufactured its products. The case went to the US Supreme Court, which ruled against the shoe company by differentiating between commercial speech and public speech, the former not having protection under the First Amendment.

When considering whether - or what - to report, think about the following:

- **Why does the company want to report?** Is the company looking to improve its reputation? Join a CSR index? Because competitors are reporting?

- **Will reporting have a negative impact?** In certain circumstances, issuing a sustainability/CSR report may weaken the company's competitive position.

- **Who is the intended audience?** Is the company most interested in engaging the public, customers, investors or NGOs? Use the answer to define what and how to report. Consider issuing a Statement of Significant Audiences and Materiality to clarify this and establish the reference point for materiality in the disclosure.

- **What story should be told?** Is the goal to communicate financial impact of sustainability/CSR efforts, focus on specific matters or to tell a general story?

- **How should it be told?** Is the story most effectively communicated by using a narrative, technical data or metrics? Should it follow a specific reporting framework for standalone sustainability/CSR reports, or will it be integrated into the financial report?

- **Should it be audited/verified?** In the US, it is not common for sustainability/CSR reports to undergo an audit. Doing so is voluntary, but may be considered worth the cost.

Climate change has become a focal point of sustainability/CSR reporting. The G20's Task Force on Climate-related Financial Disclosures (TCFD) released their reporting recommendations in June 2017. TCFD recommendations involve reporting on major themes of climate risk governance, strategy, risk management metrics and targets. One aspect of the recommendations that differs from other reporting frameworks is that TCFD intends that climate disclosures be incorporated into financial reports rather than in stand-alone sustainability/CSR reporting.

TCFD is gaining momentum. GreenBiz reported that:

> *"As of Dec. 12, an estimated 237 companies from 29 countries — with a combined market capitalization of more than $6.3 trillion (PDF) — publicly had committed to supporting the TCFD recommendations. Among them were 150 financial firms responsible for assets of $81.7 trillion, such as Bank of America, BlackRock and Citigroup."*

Today, there is more pressure related to execution of programs than reporting. GoldmanSachs reported

> *... little evidence that companies disclosing non-quantifiable policies outperform peers – in fact, in our backtest, they tend to do worse... Our work finds that disclosure alone is linked to stock underperformance (an average of 376 bps annually relative to non-disclosing sector peers). Rather it is performance on ESG factors that matters most.*

But the process of reporting can consume those involved, distracting from what is really important. Some well-known global corporations have a surprisingly weak reality behind their impressive looking reports.

Supply Chain/Supplier CSR Evaluations

Supplier CSR audits were discussed earlier, but are also a relevant squirrel. In concept, these audits are a good idea; but as with all things, the devil is in the details. Those who commission supplier audits don't typically treat the process with an appropriate level of respect. More frequently than not, pricing is the overriding factor when companies select an auditor, with audit quality and auditor competence taking a back seat. Auditors who choose to compete in this market face tough choices about scoping, staffing and evidence sampling to meet budgets, many times resulting in poor audits. At the same time, CSR auditors continue to accept engagements that they realize will produce an inferior product.

Some companies hiring CSR auditors are comfortable with the outcome only when extra money is spent for in-house staff to supervise external auditors, increasing the audit's total cost. Rather than paying for extra internal oversight of low-cost external auditors, it may be more cost-effective to simply pay a reasonable price for an appropriately designed and staffed audit in which the company trusts.

Auditing should not be considered the end game. The goal is for identified deficiencies to be corrected and eliminate environmental, social and safety risks. Unfortunately, organizations are at times more concerned with getting the audit done as part of a standard internal process than with the actual audit results.

Supplier CSR audits can be valuable if they are given due respect by buyers and executed professionally by auditors. Where these programs are done well, they garner a three-squirrel rating, but the current general approach to buying and selling the services knocks one squirrel off the limb.

APSCA

The Association of Professional Social Compliance Auditors (APSCA) is a new organization "created to enhance the professionalism, consistency, and credibility of individual auditors and organizations performing independent social compliance audits." APSCA is developing standards for CSR audit practices and a certification program for individual auditors, which were piloted in November 2017.

It is too soon to tell if APSCA will succeed; hopefully, the market will support it. But buyers will need to move from their entrenched view that CSR auditing is an undifferentiated commodity to be selected only on price.

Green Bonds

What is a green bond? There isn't an easy answer to that question, yet green bonds are growing in popularity. One article estimated that as of September 2017, approximately 1200 green bonds have been issued with an average value of US$214 million.

There are green bonds and social bonds, which are different. Green bonds as defined by the International Capital Market Association (ICMA) are bonds exclusively used to finance or refinance "green projects" - projects that address key areas of environmental concern such as climate change, natural resources depletion, loss of biodiversity, and air, water or soil pollution. There may be social co-benefits from a green bond, but the primary goal is to address environmental impacts.

Social bonds as defined by ICMA as bonds exclusively used to fund "social projects" - specific social issues or positive social outcomes "especially, but not exclusively, for a target population(s)" [sic]. There may be environmental co-benefits from a social bond, but the primary goal is to assist people directly.

Mixing a green bond with a social bond results in a sustainability bond according to IMCA. Uh, okay.

Tesla's August 2017 bond sale raised US$1.8 billion for the company. Even though Tesla as a whole is built on a platform of green products and sustainability, the company specifically avoided calling its' bonds green to the surprise of many observers. Tesla's decision may be due in part to the fact that the capital was used to expand manufacturing capabilities rather than for a "green project." Apple on the other hand has raised US$2.5 billion in two separate green bond sales. Apple didn't really need to raise capital given that it has a cash hoard of US$260 billion stuffed in its' mattress. The company chose to support the green bond market and is using the funds to finance "green projects" - energy efficiency and the development of a closed loop supply chain to increase recovery of materials from discarded electronics.

Many question whether the green bond label has value and is worth the effort, but supporters are quick to point out that issuing green bonds brings attention to companies and offerings that would otherwise go unnoticed.

SASB

The Sustainability Accounting Standards Board (SASB) is a US private nonprofit organization established in 2011. SASB is not a governmental entity, nor is the organization it tries to mirror: the US Financial Accounting Standards Board (FASB). FASB, established in 1973, is the independent, private-sector organization that establishes financial accounting and reporting standards for public and private companies following Generally Accepted Accounting Principles (GAAP). The FASB is recognized by the Securities and Exchange Commission as the designated accounting standard setter, and their standards are recognized as authoritative by state Boards of Accountancy and the American Institute of CPAs (AICPA). SASB ultimately hopes for their standards to be adopted into SEC reporting requirements.

The organization was initially underwritten by former New York City Mayor and billionaire Michael Bloomberg, and now has an impressive list of US financial luminaries on its Board including two former Chairs of the Securities and Exchange Commission. It has developed a set of "sustainability accounting standards" grouped into 79 sectors that were still draft as of December 2017. The "standards" attempt to identify aspects of company operations, management and strategy that, according to SASB, have a potential for being financially material under US securities disclosure requirements.

In April 2016, the SEC requested public comment on its Business and Financial Disclosure Requirements of Regulation S-K Concept Release. This was a comprehensive review of financial reporting elements under SEC Regulation S-K, in an attempt to modernize disclosures and seek input from the public. Sustainability disclosure was among the topics included in the Concept Release, and on which interested parties commented. Many commenters expressed concern that SASB standards were an attempt to redefine materiality. One commenter referenced in the Release stated sustainability issues "are not typically material to an understanding of the company's financial performance." The Business Roundtable, an organization of CEOs who lead companies with more than 16 million employees and more than $7 trillion in annual revenues, dedicated five pages (out of a total of seven) to explaining the importance of retaining the existing definition of materiality, and that mandated sustainability disclosures "may be of interest to some investors, but would not be material to reasonable investors as a group." Recall that the Supreme Court defined financial materiality using the "reasonable investor" as its foundation and that there are multiple possible interpretations of the phrase. As was noted in the Release, "disclosure to serve the needs of limited segments of the investing public, even if otherwise desirable, may be inappropriate."

Countervailing arguments take a position that disclosure standards should not be static but should respond to new developments in investor views of materiality.

SEC-regulated companies are already required to make materiality evaluations of their business and financials – regardless of the specific business or financial matter. If a different materiality standard or disclosure emerges, there is a risk that companies might find previous materiality evaluations inadvertently omitted sustainability matters that may be material under the current definition. This could trigger shareholder lawsuits and enforcement from the SEC. Accounting guru Baruch Lev seems to be of two minds about SASB. In discussing a panel session he participated in, he said:

> *"I did point out that the SASB approach is quite useful for investors. But the demand for voluntary disclosure by companies could create an invitation for lawsuits all*

> *over the world, if certain disclosures were*
> *made   regarding   a   company's*
> *environmental impacts."*

Early adopters and supporters of SASB - along with
service providers who stand to gain from its market
acceptance - are enthusiastic about the group and its
mission. Interestingly, there are those in the investment
community and ratings agencies who are less than fully
supportive based on my private conversations with
some industry heavy hitters. Companies themselves
express concern of technical deficiencies and the lack
of flexibility of the provisional and draft standards to
reflect circumstances unique to them: the current
exposure draft standards require (i.e., using the word
"shall") disclosure of most topics with no apparent
recognition that variances may be appropriate on a
company-by-company basis.

While the standards may provide consistency of the
universe of topics for disclosure, it remains to be seen
whether (a) the topics are truly appropriate, meaningful
or valid for their intended purpose and (b) reporting
companies will improve data quality enough to resolve
current investor concerns. The current exposure draft
standards would benefit from additional manufacturing,
operations, technical or EHS regulatory knowledge. As
they have only been used by a handful of companies
(and even then, they were in provisional draft form),
the real-world application and validity of the standards
has yet to be tested. For example, in comparing the
eleven sustainability financial materiality indicators of
RobecoSAM (used by the Dow Jones Sustainability
Indices) to SASB's eleven Sustainability Disclosure
Topics and Accounting Metrics for the pharmaceutical
industry:

- only seven SASB topics are addressed by RobecoSAM's indicators, and

- of the six indicators considered the most financially material by RobecoSAM, only three are also SASB topics – meaning the other eight SASB indicators are not considered material by RobecoSAM.

SASB launched in a sympathetic period of US policy-making. The Trump administration has already started rolling back regulations, some involving environmental, health, safety and corporate governance. The administration's position is clear on matters they consider burdensome to business. Two former SEC Directors clarified in a 2016 panel that they haven't seen much demand for such standards and no regulatory movement in that direction is anticipated. It seems unlikely that SASB will be codified anytime soon; individual companies must decide whether to adopt SASB's standards on a voluntary basis. Until sustainability accounting and disclosure standards are mandated in the US, uptake will likely be rather limited.

In addition to accounting standards, the organization offers a professional credential program called the Fundamentals of Sustainability Accounting (FSA). For individuals, pursuing this credential may be beneficial because the educational materials are interesting and useful. The credentialing and testing program was revised in late 2017 to address needed improvements from the first generation. Similar to the APSCA certification, it is not yet clear how or if the marketplace for services/employees values the credential.

SASB's usefulness and acceptance may grow in the future, but right now it may be best to take a wait and see approach.

CHAPTER 15
WRAPPED IN A BOW

This book covers much background because sustainability professionals fight daily against the historical business context of sustainability and social responsibility. Understanding why the fight exists in the first place is helpful in avoiding similar obstacles in the future, but some folks prefer to get to the point. For those, this chapter summarizes major points of the book. Although this list is ordered in a generally logical progression, using it in practice will be iterative. It is possible some steps won't apply at all in a given situation. Use this as a flexible guideline or framework, not as a rigid checklist, structure or operating procedure. I really recommend reading the book in its entirety first to understand the complete context of the summary.

Acknowledge the Credibility Gap

- There is no consensus on a clear and actionable definition of sustainability/CSR. Gain an understanding of what "sustainability" or "corporate social responsibility" means to the company. Executives tend to view sustainability in environmental terms.

- To many executives, the word sustainability is a cue to stop listening. One way to begin changing the perception of sustainability is to stop using the word.

- Short-term (i.e., quarter by quarter) management infects many C-suites, which is an obstacle to the long-term view of sustainability. This can be exceptionally challenging to sustainability/CSR practitioners since executives are frequently personally compensated for quarterly financial performance. In these situations, credibility of the sustainability/CSR organization, leader and project justification is crucial.

- Use simple and jargon-free language. Framing sustainability appropriately to executives is a prerequisite to communicating facts and nudging toward the desired outcome.

- The internal perception of sustainability's place in the org chart, its leader and staff can predetermine a program's destiny. If the program is seen as an important part of the company, the pressure is on to retain that respect. Otherwise, time must be spent building credibility before perception changes.

Identifying Opportunities

- A sustainability/CSR opportunity can be presented either as a risk management tool or as business improvement. Humans are psychologically biased to avoid risk, but it may be better to frame the opportunity in positive terms. You will need to assess the best direction for your audience.

- When presenting options for consumers or executives, apply choice architecture to reduce - or maximize - desired bias and behavior in the outcome. Make it easy for them to choose the best outcome.

- To the extent possible, align sustainability/CSR opportunities with the company's core competency and traditional product offerings. This makes it easy for executives to see how the company's specific capabilities are relevant and how profit can be generated.

- Understand customers' key buying criteria, and how their perceptions of sustainability impact their decisions. Be skeptical of customer survey results as they may not reflect the reality of consumer buying behavior or priorities. Social media can be leveraged to identify unbiased customer feedback in real time.

- Large companies are generally leading sustainability/CSR program implementation, but there are millions of smaller companies that can generate real financial benefits too.

Financial Valuations

- Given the credibility gap faced by sustainability practitioners, financial valuations of opportunities must be reasonable. Over-reaching and over-promising adds fuel to credibility problems. Biases turn into obstacles when we try to force a solution or valuation where one may not exist, or is inappropriate - destroying credibility.

- Part of establishing and maintaining the foundation of credibility is using good information and data. It must be defensible, reliable, verifiable and possibly corroborated by a credible entity.

- Linking sustainability/CSR improvements to stock prices can be a minefield. It is probably best to avoid that and focus on revenues, cash flow, margins, operating cost reductions, customer requirements and market access.

- In the US, the Securities and Exchange Commission is monitoring non-GAAP financial disclosures, meaning sustainability/CSR valuations in financial reports should be supported with credible processes, assumptions and data.

- Consider implications of disclosing innovations in sustainability/CSR reporting. Maximizing profits may involve reducing transparency in order to maintain the exclusivity of those innovations. At the same time, transparency may please investors, possibly contributing to improved stock prices.

Supply Chains

- Today's manufacturing business model presents the sustainability/CSR professionals' biggest challenge. A manufacturer's influence - and corporate sustainability/CSR - extends backwards into a company's supply chain and forward to a product's disposal or recycling.

Manufacturers have minimal influence beyond their direct suppliers. Imposing sustainability/CSR requirements on suppliers can increase costs.

- Supply chain sustainability initiatives may force US cultural expectations on centuries of local culture where suppliers/contract manufacturers operate. This should be a consideration when seeking to change behaviors or expectations through a company's supply chain.

- Current CSR audit price points are a major driver of audit quality, or lack thereof. Brands and factories share blame for poor CSR audits because they establish scopes, hire auditors and set market prices.

- Supplier audits have little value if audit findings are not corrected.

Sustainability/CSR Reporting

- Sustainability/CSR reporting is worthless when the report is sole - or primary - outcome of the company's activities. Pretty reports with pictures of trees, butterflies and children are outdated and should be avoided. Emphasize program execution over reporting.

- Consider the following:
  - Why report?
  - Who is the intended audience?
  - What story should be told?
  - How should it be told?
  - Does it need assurance/verification?

- Define a specific intended audience for the report and make that audience the nucleus around which the report is crafted. The Board of Directors can formalize and publish a statement of the report's intended audience. This clarifies the basis on which the company determined materiality.

Chasing Squirrels

- Chasing sustainability/CSR squirrels may not be worth the effort. Squirrels of sustainability include new fads, reporting guidelines, fantastic claims of financial value, as well as customer requirements. Some sustainability squirrels are worth catching, others, perhaps not. Sustainability practitioners should critically evaluate each and make the appropriate determination.

* * *

Sustainability/CSR practitioners need to watch for new developments in accounting, business, economics, behavioral science and societal trends. Leveraging new ideas and tactics can be tools for building programs and initiatives. In a perfect world, sustainability and corporate social responsibility would be so deeply integrated into company strategy, products and operations that it would not be distinct or identifiable. There are companies who are already there. If more companies do that, sustainability will be dead. And that would be good.

REFERENCES

Reference materials below are mentioned within the text or were used in the research for the book.

Addady, M. (2016, January 20). This is Why Costco's Slavery Lawsuit Was Dismissed. *Fortune.* Retrieved from http://fortune.com/2016/01/20/costco-slavery-lawsuit/

American Chemistry Council. (n.d.) Responsible Care. Retrieved from https://responsiblecare.americanchemistry.com

Arthur D. Little. (n.d.). Homepage. Retrieved from http://www.adlittle.com

Association of Certified Fraud Examiners (ACFE). (n.d.). The Fraud Triangle. Retrieved from http://www.acfe.com/fraud-triangle.aspx.

Association of Professional Social Compliance Auditors. (n.d.). Homepage. Retrieved from http://www.theapsca.org

Baaz, M.E., Gondola, D., Marijnen, E., & Verweijen, J. (2015, March 5). Virunga's white savior complex: How the film distorts the politics and people of Congo. *Foreign Affairs.* Retrieved from https://www.foreignaffairs.com/articles/africa/ 2015-03-05/virungas-white-savior-complex

Bailey, J. & Koller, T. (2017, June). Sustainability and Rewriting the Book on Valuation: An Interview with Tim Koller. *Journal of Applied Corporate Finance,* 29: 16–20. Retrieved from http://dx.doi.org/10.1111/jacf.12229

Bajaj, J. (2015, December 17). Why the definition of sustainability must change. [Blog post]. *Mother*

Nature Network. Retrieved from https://www.mnn.com/home-blog/guest-columnist/blogs/why-definition-sustainability-must-change

Balcon, T. (2015, December 3). CEO – Chief environmental officers. *Chief Executive Officer.* Retrieved from http://www.the-chiefexecutive.com/features/featureceo-chief-environmental-officers-4785394/

Barre, J. (2017, November 10). The current state and evolution of corporate sustainability assessment organizations. *Sustainable Brands.* Retrieved from http://www.sustainablebrands.com/news_and_views /marketing_comms/juliette_barre/current_state_evo lution_sustainability_assessing_organ

Barton, D., Manyika, J. & Williamson, S.K. (2017, January 9). Finally, Evidence that Managing for the Long Term Pays Off. *Harvard Business Review.* Retrieved from https://hbr.org/2017/02/finally-proof-that-managing-for-the-long-term-pays-off

Beaumont, P. (2013, June 5). 5 Definitions of Sustainability. [Blog post]. *The Green Dandelion, The University of Rochester.* Retrieved from http://blogs.rochester.edu/thegreendandelion/2013/ 06/5-definitions-of-sustainability/

Blanding, M. (2016, September 12). How big brands should monitor factory conditions in their supply chains. *Forbes.* Retrieved from https://www.forbes.com/sites/hbsworkingknowledge /2016/09/12/how-big-brands-should-monitor-factory-conditions-in-their-supply-chains/#1507db13796d

Blasco, J.L., & King, A. (2017). The road ahead: The KPMG Survey of Corporate Responsibility reporting 2017. *KPMG International Cooperative.* Retrieved from

https://home.kpmg.com/content/dam/kpmg/campai
gns/csr/pdf/CSR_Reporting_2017.pdf

Bloomberg. (2017, November 2). *Full show: What'd you miss?* [Video file]. Retrieved from https://www.bloomberg.com/news/videos/2017-11-02/full-show-what-d-you-miss-11-02-video

Board of Environmental, Health & Safety Auditor Certifications. (n.d.). Homepage. Retrieved from https://na.theiia.org/certification/BEAC/Pages/defa ult.aspx

Boerner, H. (2017, July 17). Conversation with Professor Baruch Lev at NYU: Is Accounting Outmoded? [Blog post]. *Governance & Accountability Institute's sustainabilityupdate.* Retrieved from https://ga-institute.com/Sustainability-Update/2017/07/18/conversation-with-professor-baruch-lev-at-nyu-is-accounting-outmoded/

Bonini, S., Görner, S., Jones, A., & Ballek, M. (2010, March). How companies manage sustainability: McKinsey Global Survey results. *McKinsey & Company.* Retrieved from https://www.mckinsey.com/business-functions/sustainability-and-resource-productivity/our-insights/how-companies-manage-sustainability-mckinsey-global-survey-results

Bové, A-T., & Swartz, S. (2016, November). Starting at the source: Sustainability in supply chains. *McKinsey & Company.* Retrieved from https://www.mckinsey.com/business-functions/sustainability-and-resource-productivity/our-insights/starting-at-the-source-sustainability-in-supply-chains

Bové, A-T., D'Herde, D., & Swartz, S. (2017, December). Sustainability's deepening imprint. *McKinsey & Company.* Retrieved from https://www.mckinsey.com/ business-functions/sustainability-and-resource-productivity/our-insights/sustainabilitys-deepening-imprint

Bower, J.L. & Paine, L.S. (2017). The Error at the Heart of Corporate Leadership. *Harvard Business Review: Managing for the Long Term*. Retrieved from https://hbr.org/2017/05/managing-for-the-long-term#the-error-at-the-heart-of-corporate-leadership

Boyd, T. (2017, October 31). Larry Fink says Blackrock will take activism to a 'whole new level'. *Financial Review*. Retrieved from http://www.afr.com/business/larry-fink-says-blackrock-will-take-activism-to-a-whole-new-level-20171031-gzc2lt

Broadstock, D. (2017, September 22). Going green: the changing face of corporate finance. *South China Morning Post*. Retrieved from http://www.scmp.com/business/banking-finance/article/2112354/going-green-changing-face-corporate-finance

Brown, A. (2016, May 9). There could be problems for a bunch of companies trying to be the "Uber for gas." [Blog post]. *Business Insider*. Retrieved from http://www.businessinsider.com/on-demand-gas-apps-scrutinized-2016-5

Cahill, L.B., & Kane, R.W. (1989). *Environmental Audits*. Government Institutes Inc. Rockville, MA.

Carson, R., & Darling, L. (1962). *Silent spring*. Boston: Houghton Mifflin.

CDP. (n.d.). Homepage. Retrieved from https://www.cdp.net/en

Chasan, E. (2017, December 8). BlackRock wields its $6 trillion club to combat climate risks. *Bloomberg*. Retrieved from https://www.bloomberg.com/news/articles/2017-12-08/blackrock-wields-its-6-trillion-club-to-combat-climate-risks

Chen, J. (2018, January 4). Markets Fairly Grade Share Buybacks. *CFO.* Retrieved from http://ww2.cfo.com/investor-relations-banking-capital-markets/2018/01/markets-fairly-grade-share-buybacks/

Chitnis, S. (2016, July 13). Sizing the market for US B2B companies in 7 charts [Blog post]. *Insights.* Retrieved from https://www.compile.com/blog/insights/sizing-us-b2b-market-7-charts/

Clark, G.L., Feiner, A., & Viehs, M. (2014, September). From the Stockholder to the Stakeholder, How Sustainability Can Drive Financial Outperformance. *University of Oxford and Arabesque Partners.* Retrieved from http://www.smithschool.ox.ac.uk/publications/reports/SSEE_Arabesque_Paper_16Sept14.pdf

Climate Central. (n.d.). Gallery. Retrieved from http://www.climatecentral.org/gallery/graphics/transportation-is-the-biggest-source-of-us-emissions

Davis-Peccoud, J., Stone, P. & Tovey, C. (2016, November 18). Achieving Breakthrough Results in Sustainability. *Bain & Company Bain Brief.* Retrieved from http://www.bain.com/publications/articles/achieving-breakthrough-results-in-sustainability.aspx

de Freytas-Tamura, K. (2018, January 11). Plastics Pile Up as China Refuses to Take the West's Recycling. *The New York Times.* Retrieved from https://www.nytimes.com/2018/01/11/world/china-recyclables-ban.html?_r=0

Denning, S. (2017, April 27). *The 'Pernicious Nonsense' of Maximizing Shareholder Value.* Retrieved from https://www.forbes.com/sites/stevedenning/2017/04/27/harvard-business-review-the-pernicious-nonsense-of-maximizing-shareholder-value/#4311845171f0

Derrien, F., Frésard, L., Slabik, V. & Valta, P. (2017, October 3). The Negative Effects of Mergers and Acquisitions on the Value of Rivals. HEC Paris Research Paper No. FIN-2017-1204. Retrieved from https://ssrn.com/abstract=2960576

DesMarais, C. (2016, August 8). Here's How Much People Like Their Subscription Boxes (Infographic). [Blog post]. *Inc.* Retrieved from https://www.inc.com/christina-desmarais/heres-data-showing-the-crazy-growth-of-subscription-box-services-infographic.html

Dodd-Frank Wall Street Reform and Consumer Protection Act, Pub. L. No. 111-203, § 929-Z, 124 Stat. 1376, 1871 (2010) (codified at 15 U.S.C. § 780)

Eccles, R.G. & Youmans, T. (2015). *Materiality in corporate governance: The statement of significant audiences and materiality* (Working Paper No. 16-023). Retrieved from http://www.hbs.edu/faculty/Publication%20Files/16-023_f29dce5d-cbac-4840-8d5f-32b21e6f644e.pdf

Elm Sustainability Partners. (2014, April 1). SEC Commissioner Speaks to Accountability for Sustainability Accounting. [Blog post] http://www.elmsustainability.com/sec-commissioner-speaks-accountability-sustainability-accounting/

Elm Sustainability Partners. (2015, April 21). Sustainability is Stupid. [Blog post]. http://www.elmsustainability.com/sustainability-is-stupid/

Elm Sustainability Partners. (2016, June 3). "Too Many Sustainability Standards" No Longer a Solo Chorus.   [Blog   post].

http://www.elmsustainability.com/too-many-sustainability-standards-no-longer-a-solo-chorus/

Elm Sustainability Partners. (2016, August 1). Is Social Auditing Really Auditing? [Blog post]. http://www.elmsustainability.com/is-social-auditing-really-auditing/

Elm Sustainability Partners. (2017, November 3). Predicting the failure – or success – of sustainability leadership. Retrieved from http://www.elmsustainability.com/ predicting-the-failure-or-success-of-sustainability-leadership/

European Commission. (2017). Information from European union institutions, bodies, offices and agencies. *Official Journal of the European Union.* Retrieved from http://eur-lex.europa.eu/legal-content/EN/TXT/PDF/?uri=CELEX:52017XC070 5 (01)&from=EN

Fan, X. (2015). The measurement of Schumpeterian profits in pollution-intensive industries under the environmental regulation. *CNKI.* Retrieved from http://en.cnki.com.cn/Article_en/CJFDTotal-ZGKT201503011.htm

Federal Trade Commission. (n.d.). Green Guides Homepage. Retrieved from https://www.ftc.gov/news-events/media-resources/truth-advertising/green-guides

Feldman, S.J., Soyka, P.A., & Ameer, P.G. (1997, November). Does Improving a Firm's Environmental Management System and Environmental Performance Result in a Higher Stock Price? *The Journal of Investing.* Retrieved from http://joi.iijournals.com/content/6/4/87

Financial Accounting Standards Board (FASB). (n.d.). Homepage. Retrieved from http://www.fasb.org

Financial Times. (2017, November 15). Banks help to bring climate change for green bonds. Retrieved from https://www.ft.com/content/2f7739da-c9f1-11e7-aa33-c63fdc9b8c6c

Fink, L. (2018). Larry Fink's Annual Letter to CEOs: A Sense of Purpose. *BlackRock, Inc.* Retrieved from https://www.blackrock.com/corporate/en-us/investor-relations/larry-fink-ceo-letter

Finnegan, B. (2014). Responsibility outsourced: Social audits, workplace certification and twenty years of failure to protect worker rights. *The American Federation of Labor-Congress of Industrial Organizations.* Retrieved from https://aflcio.org/sites/default/files/2017-03/CSReport.pdf

Friedman, M. (1970, September 13). The social responsibility of business is to increase its profits. *The New York Times Magazine.* Retrieved from http://www.umich.edu/~thecore/doc/Friedman.pdf

Giese, G., Lee, L-E., Meals, D., Nagy, Z. & Nishikawa, L. (2017, November). Foundations of ESG Investing, Part 1: How ESG Affects Equity Valuation, Risk and Performance. *MSCI ESG Research LLC.* Retrieved from https://www.savvyinvestor.net/sites/default/files/node/paper/file/Foundations%20of%20ESG%20Investing.pdf

Global Reporting Initiative. (2018, January 10). Improve the quality of your report with GRI's new Disclosure Review Service. *GRI.* Retrieved from https://www.globalreporting.org/information/news-and-press-center/Pages/Improve-the-quality-of-your-report-with-GRI's-new-Disclosure-Review-Service.aspx

Griffin, P.A., Lont, D.H. & Sun, E. (2013, August 11). Supply Chain Sustainability: Evidence on Conflict Minerals. *Pacific Accounting Review DOI: 10.1108/PAR-04-2013-0023.* https://ssrn.com/abstract=2129371.

GS Sustain. (2017, April 18). The PM's Guide to the ESG Revolution. *The Goldman Sachs Group, Inc.* Retrieved from https://www.gsam.com/content/dam/gsam/pdfs/inte rnational/en/institutions/articles/2017/GS_Sustain_ The_PMs_Guide_to_the_ESG_Revolution.pdf?sa =n&rd=n

Harper, D. (n.d.). EVA: What Does It Really Mean? Investopedia Academy. Retrieved from https://www.investopedia.com/university/eva/eva5.a sp

Heim, L. (2002, October 17). *Competitive Advantage: Using EHS in Value Chains.* Presented at NAEM 10th Annual Environmental Management Forum. https://www.slideshare.net/lheim/LHeim-NAEM-Value-Chain

Hess, D., & Dunfee, T.W. (2007). The Kasky-Nike threat to corporate social reporting: Implementing a standard of optimal truthful disclosure as a solution. *Business Ethics Quarterly, 17*(1), 5-32. https://doi.org/10.5840/beq200717119

Higgins, K., White, J., Beller, A., & Shapiro, M. (2017, June). The SEC and Improving Sustainability Reporting. *Journal of Applied Corporate Finance.* Retrieved from http://onlinelibrary.wiley.com/doi/10.1111/jacf.122 30/full

Housel, M. (2017, June 30). The Best Simple Business Models. [Blog post]. *Collaborative Fund.* Retrieved from http://www.collaborativefund.com/blog/simple-business-models-that-work/

Huber, B.M. & Comstock, M. (2017, July 27). ESG Reports and Ratings: What They Are, Why They Matter. *Harvard Law School Forum on Corporate Governance and Financial Regulation.* Retrieved from https://corpgov.law.harvard.edu/2017/07/27/esg-reports-and-ratings-what-they-are-why-they-matter/

ICMA. (2017). *The green bond principles 2017*. Paris, FR: *ICMA Paris*. Retrieved from https://www.icmagroup.org/assets/documents/Regulatory/Green-Bonds/GreenBondsBrochure-JUNE2017.pdf

ICMA. (2017). *The social bond principles 2017*. Paris, FR: *ICMA Paris*. Retrieved from https://www.icmagroup.org/assets/documents/Regulatory/Green-Bonds/SocialBondsBrochure-JUNE2017.pdf

Institute of Environmental Management & Assessment (iema). (n.d.). Homepage. Retrieved from https://www.iema.net

Institute of Environmental Management & Assessment (iema). (2013, May 16). EMS audits assuring compliance 'long way off'. *Transform*. Retrieved from https://transform.iema.net/article/ems-audits-assuring-compliance-'long-way-off'

Institute of Internal Auditors. (n.d.). Environmental Health & Safety Audit Center. Retrieved from https://www.theiia.org/centers/ehsac/Pages/default.aspx

International Organization for Standardization (n.d.). ISO 14000 family – Environmental management. https://www.iso.org/iso-14001-environmental-management.html

International Renewable Energy Agency (IRENA). (2018, January). Renewable Power Generation Costs in 2017. Retrieved from https://cms.irena.org/publications/2018/Jan/Renewable-power-generation-costs-in-2017

Investopedia. (n.d.). What is 'Alpha'. *Investopedia*. Retrieved from https://www.investopedia.com/terms/a/alpha.asp

Investopedia. (n.d.). What is 'Volatility'. *Investopedia.* Retrieved from https://www.investopedia.com/terms/v/volatility.asp

John, A. (2014, June 30). Our nation's river: A troubled past, a bright future. *Potomac Conservancy.* Retrieved from https://potomac.org/blog/2014/6/27/dc-water-troubled-past-bright-future

Journal of Applied Corporate Finance. (2017, Spring). *The SEC and Improving Sustainability Reporting.* New Jersey: John Wiley & Sons.

Journal of Applied Corporate Finance. (2017, Spring). *Sustainability and Rewriting the Book on Valuation: An Interview with Tim Koller.* New Jersey: John Wiley & Sons.

Journal of Applied Corporate Finance. (2017, Spring). *The Next Wave of ESG Integration: Lessons from Institutional Investors.* New Jersey: John Wiley & Sons.

K., K. (2017, July 4). What makes bonds "green"? Simply using the proceeds for environmentally friendly investments is not enough. *The Economist.* Retrieved from https://www.economist.com/blogs/economist-explains/2017/07/economist-explains-1

Katz, M. (2017, December 28). CalPERS Calls ESG Criticism 'Laughable'. *chief investment officer.* Retrieved from https://www.ai-cio.com/news/calpers-calls-esg-criticism-laughable/

Khalamayzer, A. (2018, January 9). Why voluntary climate risk disclosure is going mainstream. *GreenBiz.* Retrieved from https://www.greenbiz.com/article/why-voluntary-climate-risk-disclosure-going-mainstream

Khan, M.N., Serafeim, G., & Yoon, A. (2015). *Corporate sustainability: First evidence on materiality* (Working Paper No. 15-073). Retrieved from

https://dash.harvard.edu/bitstream/handle/1/14369
106/15-073.pdf?sequence=1

Kim, A. (2016, July 21). Comments on business and financial disclosure requirements of regulation S-K concept release, file number S7-06-16. *Elm Sustainability Partners*. Retrieved from https://www.sec.gov/comments/s7-06-16/s70616-307.pdf

Kleiman, J. (n.d.). Love canal: A brief history. *Geneseo*. https://www.geneseo.edu/history/love_canal_history

Koller, T., Goedhart, M., & Wessels, D. (2015). *Valuation: Measuring and Managing the Value of Companies, Sixth Edition*. New Jersey: John Wiley & Sons.

Koons, C. & Langreth, R. (2017, December 20). The Loopholes Drug Companies Use to Keep Prices High. *Bloomberg News*. Retrieved from https://www.bloomberg.com/news/features/2017-12-20/the-loopholes-drug-companies-use-to-keep-prices-high

Krut, R. & Gleckman, H. (1998). *ISO14001: A Missed Opportunity for Sustainable Global Industrial Development*. London: Earthscan Publications.

Lakoff, G. (2014). *The All New Don't Think of an Elephant! Know your values and frame the debate*. White River Junction, VT: Chelsea Green Publishing.

Lammers, L. (2011, January 5). Sustainability named one of 'jargoniest jargon' words of 2010 by Ad Age. *Triple Pundit*. Retrieved from https://www.triplepundit.com/2011/01/ad-age-names-sustainability-one-jargoniest-jargon-words-2010/

Latson, J. (2015, June 22). The burning river that sparked a revolution. *Time Magazine*. Retrieved from http://time.com/3921976/cuyahoga-fire/

Lazonick, W. (2017, August 8). How "shareholder value" is killing innovation. *Harvard Law School Forum on Corporate Governance and Financial Regulation.* Retrieved from https://corpgov.law.harvard.edu/2017/08/08/how-shareholder-value-is-killing-innovation/

Lazonick, W. (2017, June). The functions of the stock market and the fallacies of shareholder value (Working Paper No. 58). Retrieved from https://www.ineteconomics.org/research/research-papers/the-functions-of-the-stock-market-and-the-fallacies-of-shareholder-value

Lev, B. (2012) *Winning Investors Over: Surprising Truths About Honesty, Earnings Guidance, and Other Ways to Boost Your Stock Price.* (Kindle Edition). Boston: Harvard Business Review Press.

Lev, B. & Feng, G. (2016). *The End of Accounting and the Path Forward for Investors and Managers* (Kindle edition). New Jersey: John Wiley & Sons, Inc.

Lev, B. (2017, June). Evaluating Sustainable Competitive Advantage. *Journal of Applied Corporate Finance,* 29: 70–75. doi:10.1111/jacf.12234

Lev, B. (2017, December 14). Corporate Financial Reporting: Facts or Fiction? *Lev End of Accounting Blog.* Retrieved from https://levtheendofaccountingblog.wordpress.com/2017/12/14/12-1-17-new-corporate-financial-reporting-facts-or-fiction/

Lev, B. (2017, December 20). Intangible assets are changing investment. *Lev End of Accounting Blog.* Retrieved from https://levtheendofaccountingblog.wordpress.com/2017/12/20/12-20-17-new-intangible-assets-are-changing-investment/

Lin, B., Romero, S., Jeffers, A., DeGaetano, L. & Aquilino, F. (2017, July). Are Sustainability

Rankings Consistent Across Ratings Agencies? *The CPA Journal.* Retrieved from https://www.cpajournal.com/2017/07/19/sustainabili ty-rankings-consistent-across-ratings-agencies/

Luchs, M.G., Naylor, R.W., Irwin, J.R., & Raghunathan, R. (2010). The sustainability liability: Potential negative effects of ethicality on product preference. *Journal of Marketing,* 74(5), 18-31. https://doi.org/10.1509/jmkg.74.5.18

Lyons, D. (2009, December 24). "We Start With the Customer and We Work Backward" Jeff Bezos on Amazon's Success. *Slate.* Retrieved from http://www.slate.com/articles/news_and_politics/ne wsmakers/2009/12/we_start_with_the_customer_an d_we_work_backward.html

Matthiesen, M-L. & Salzmann, A.J., (2017). Corporate social responsibility and firms' cost of equity: how does culture matter? *Cross Cultural & Strategic Management,* Vol. 24 Issue: 1. Retrieved from https://doi.org/10.1108/CCSM-11-2015-0169

McCann, D. (2017, December 18). Investors Speak: Down With GAAP!. *CFO Magazine.* Retrieved from http://ww2.cfo.com/gaap-ifrs/2017/12/investors-speak-gaap/

Natural Resource Defense Council. (2015, August 13). The story of Silent Spring. Retrieved from https://www.nrdc.org/stories/story-silent-spring

McCann, D. (2018, January 9). To Make More Money, CEOs Harm Company Value. *CFO Magazine.* Retrieved from http://ww2.cfo.com/compensation/2018/01/to-make-more-money-ceos-harm-company-value-ceo-equity/

McNabb, F.W. (2017, August 31). An open letter to directors of public companies worldwide. *The Vanguard Group, Inc.* Retrieved from https://about.vanguard.com/investment-stewardship/governance-letter-to-companies.pdf

Newsweek. (2018, January 3). Green Ranking 2017. Retrieved from http://www.newsweek.com/green-rankings-2017-18

Nordhaus, W.D. (2004). *Economic fluctuations and growth, productivity, innovation, and entrepreneurship* (Working Paper No. 10433). Cambridge, MA: National Bureau of Economic Research. Retrieved from http://www.nber.org/papers/w10433.pdf

Nudge. (n.d.). Homepage. Retrieved from www.nudges.org

OECD (2017), "The Future of Global Value Chains: "Business as Usual" or "A New Normal"?, Directorate for Science, Technology and Innovation Policy Note, September 2017. https://www.oecd.org/sti/ind/global-value-chains.htm

Ohio History Connection. (n.d.). Cuyahoga River Fire. Retrieved from http://www.ohiohistorycentral.org/w/Cuyahoga_River_Fire

Paris, C. (2014, June 30). Exclusive: ISO 9001 certificate mills tried to literally certify cement life jackets. *Oxebridge Quality Resources International.* Retrieved from https://www.oxebridge.com/emma/exclusive-iso-9001-certificate-mills-tried-to-literally-certify-cement-life-jackets/

Porter, M.E. (1998). *Competitive Advantage: Creating and Sustaining Superior Performance: with a new introduction.* New York: Free Press.

Porter, M.E. (1998). *On Competition.* Boston: Harvard Business School Press.

Porter, M.E., & van der Linde, C. (1995). Green and competitive: Ending the stalemate. *Harvard*

Business Review. Retrieved from https://hbr.org/1995/09/green-and-competitive-ending-the-stalemate

Principles for Responsible Investment (PRI). (n.d.). Homepage. Retrieved from https://www.unpri.org/about

Principles for Responsible Investment (PRI). (2017, December). Working Towards a Sustainable Financial System: Investment Consultant Services Review. Retrieved from https://www.unpri.org/news/pri-publishes-investment-consultant-services-review

PwC. (2017, June). TCFD Final Report: A summary for business leaders. Retrieved from www.pwc.co.uk.

Raman, A. (2011, December 1). Beware of Short-term Management, Not the Short-term Investor. [Blog post]. *Harvard Business Review, HBR Online Forum The CEO's Role in Fixing the System.* Retrieved from https://hbr.org/2011/12/beware-of-the-short-term-opera.html

Rogers, G. (2017, November 20). The GAAP in ESG. Retrieved from https://www.linkedin.com/pulse/gaap-esg-greg-rogers/

Rogers, G. (2017, September 11). Why the oil industry cannot afford to retire... yet!. Retrieved from https://www.linkedin.com/pulse/why-oil-industry-cannot-afford-retire-yet-greg-rogers/

Rothman, L. (2017, March 22). Here's why the Environmental Protection Agency was created. *Time Magazine.* Retrieved from http://time.com/4696104/environmental-protection-agency-1970-history/

Ruggie, J.G. (2014, November 13). *From Audit to Innovation.* Keynote address at the Annual Conference of the Business Social Compliance Initiative. Brussels, Belgium. Retrieved from https://www.hks.harvard.edu/sites/default/files/cente rs/mrcbg/programs/cri/files/BSCI%2BKeynote.pdf

Ryan, L. (2018, January 5). Ten Business Buzzwords That Make You Sound Like An Idiot. [Blog post]. *Forbes.* Retrieved from https://www.forbes.com/sites/lizryan/2018/01/05/ten -business-buzzwords-that-make-you-sound-like-an-idiot

Shriber, T. (2018, January 2). Goldman Throws Its Hat in the ESG Ring. *Investopedia.* Retrieved from https://www.investopedia.com/news/goldman-throws-its-hat-esg-ring/

State of California Department of Justice. (n.d.). The California Transparency in Supply Chains Act. https://oag.ca.gov/SB657

Shift. (n.d.). The reporting exchange: World Business Council for Sustainable Development (WBCSD). Retrieved from https://shift.tools/resources/1418

Souder, D, Reilly, G. & Ranucci, R. (2015). Bringing Long-Term Thinking into Business. *Network for Business Sustainability Canada.* Retrieved from https://swift.van2.auro.io:8081/swift/v1/6bda5a38d0 d7490e81ba33fbb4be21dd/sophia/blox/assets/data/ 000/000/177/original/NBS-Long-Term-Thinking-SR.pdf?1492528829

Stern Value Management. (n.d.). Economic Value Added [Homepage]. http://www.eva.com

Stevens, L., & Phillips, E.E. (2017, December 20). Amazon puzzles over the perfect fit – in boxes: Padded envelopes and smaller product packaging aim to cut down on shipments with half-empty boxes. *The Wall Street Journal.* Retrieved from https://www.wsj.com/articles/amazon-aims-for-one-box-fits-all-1513765800

Stoknes, P.E. (2015). *What we think about when we try not to think about global warming: Toward a new psychology of climate action*. White River Junction, VT: Chelsea Green Publishing.

Stoknes, P.E. (2017, September). *How to transform apocalypse fatigue into action on global warming* [Video file]. Retrieved from https://www.ted.com/talks/per_espen_stoknes_how_to_transform_apocalypse_fatigue_into_action_on_global_warming

Stout, L. (2016, March 15). The Dumbest Business Idea Ever. The Myth of Maximizing Shareholder Value. *evonomics.com*. Retrieved from http://evonomics.com/maximizing-shareholder-value-dumbest-idea/

Sustainable Insight Capital Management. (2016, February). Who are the ESG rating agencies? *Sustainable Perspective for the Mainstream Investor*. Retrieved from https://www.sicm.com/docs/who-rates.pdf

Sustainability Accounting Standards Board (SASB). (n.d.). Homepage. Retrieved from https://www.sasb.org.

Sustainability Accounting Standards Board (SASB). (2017, October). Biotechnology & Pharmaceuticals Sustainability Accounting Standard, Proposed Changes to Provisional Standards, Exposure Draft, Redline of Standard for Public Comment. Retrieved from https://www.sasb.org/wp-content/uploads/2017/09/HealthCare-ExposureDraft-Redline.pdf

Sustainopia. (2017, October). Boston Program Agenda. Retrieved from http://www.sustainatopia.com/boston2017/wp-content/uploads/2017/03/2017-Boston-Agenda-3.pdf

Talks at Google. (2015, June 3). *Richard Thaler: "Misbehaving: The making of behavioral economics"* [Video file]. Retrieved from https://www.youtube.com/watch?v=42qbHeFxdzE

Thaler, R.H. (1988), Anomalies, The Winner's Curse. *Journal of Economic Perspectives.* Retrieved from https://faculty.chicagobooth.edu/richard.thaler/rese arch/pdf/the%20winner%27s%20curse.pdf

Thaler, R.H. & Sunstein, C.R. (2009). *Nudge: Improving decisions about health, wealth, and happiness.* New York, NY: Penguin Group.

Thaler, R.H. (2016). *Misbehaving: The making of behavioral economics.* New York, NY: W. W. Norton & Company.

The European Parliament and the Council of the European Union. (2005, January 7). Directive 2000/53/EC of the European Parliament and of the council. Retrieved from http://eur-lex.europa.eu/LexUriServ/LexUriServ.do?uri=CO NSLEG: 2000L0053:20050701:EN:PDF

The Republic. (2016, August 1). *Milton Friedman best moments* [Video file]. Retrieved from https://www.youtube.com/watch?v=3kx__dnAWqQ

Traves, L.S. (2009, June). The ISO 14001 Fallacy: Certification is not Compliance. *AWMA 102nd Annual Conference & Exhibition.* Retrieved at http://lmgweb.com/attachments/042_2009-A-652AWMA%20_ISO_14001%20.pdf

Triple Pundit Contributor. (2016, June 2). Is competition between sustainability reporting standards healthy? Retrieved from http://www.triplepundit.com/2016/06/ competition-sustainability-reporting-standards-healthy/

TSC Industries, Inc. v. Northway, Inc., 426 U.S. 438 (1976). (96 S.Ct. 2126, 48 L.Ed.2d 757

United Kingdom National Archives (2015, March 26). Modern Slavery Act 2015, 2015 c. 30. Retrieved from

http://www.legislation.gov.uk/ukpga/2015/30/conten
ts/enacted

United Nations. (n.d.). Sustainable development goals: 17
goals to transform our world. Retrieved from
http://www.un.org/sustainabledevelopment/sustaina
ble-development-goals/

United States Department of Labor, Bureau of
International Affairs. (n.d.). Child Labor in the
Production of Cocoa. Retrieved from
https://www.dol.gov/sites/default/files/documents/ila
b/CLCCG%202016%20Annual%20Report.pdf

United States Environmental Protection Agency. (n.d.).
Superfund: CERCLA overview. Retrieved from
https://www.epa.gov/superfund/superfund-cercla-
overview

United States Environmental Protection Agency. (n.d.).
Design for the Environmental Programs, Initiatives,
and   Projects.
·https://www.epa.gov/saferchoice/design-
environment-programs-initiatives-and-projects

United States Securities and Exchange Commission.
(2016, April 13). Business and Financial Disclosure
Required by Regulation S-K. Concept release.
Retrieved   from
https://www.sec.gov/rules/concept/2016/33-
10064.pdf

Winerip, M. (2013, September, 23). The death and
afterlife of thalidomide. *The New York Times.*
Retrieved   from
http://www.nytimes.com/2013/09/23/booming/the-
death-and-afterlife-of-thalidomide.html

Winston, A. (2018, January 19). Does Wall Street Finally
Care About Sustainability? [Blog post]. *Harvard
Business Review.* Retreived from
https://hbr.org/2018/01/does-wall-street-finally-care-
about-

sustainability?utm_campaign=hbr&utm_source=lin kedin&utm_medium=social

World Economic Forum. (2018). The Global Risks Report 2018, 13th Edition. Retrieved from http://www3.weforum.org/docs/WEF_GRR18_Rep ort.pdf

Yang, J.L. (2013, August 26). Maximizing shareholder value: The goal that changed corporate America. *The Washington Post.* Retrieved from https://www.washingtonpost.com/business/economy /maximizing-shareholder-value-the-goal-that-changed-corporate-america/2013/08/26/26e9ca8e-ed74-11e2-9008-61e94a7ea20d_story.html

Zou, J.J & Young, C. (2017, December 12). Venue of Last Resort: Wave of climate lawsuits threatens the future of Big Oil. *The Center of Public Integrity.* Retrieved from https://apps.publicintegrity.org/united-states-of-petroleum/venue-of-last-resort

ABOUT THE AUTHOR

Lawrence M. Heim, CPEA has spent almost 35 years in corporate environmental management and sustainability as in-house or external advisor to Fortune 500 and privately held multinationals in diverse industries and geographies. Frequently speaking out against groupthink in the sustainability/CSR advisory community, he has given hundreds of talks on sustainability, supply chain matters and auditing. He has provided input to the US Securities and Exchange Commission, US Department of State, US Government Accountability Office, US Department of Commerce, the Organization for Economic Cooperation and Development (OECD), and industry associations in primary metals, electronics and auditing. Today he is Managing Director of Elm Sustainability Partners, LLC and continues to work with companies on a variety of sustainability, supply chain and environmental matters.

Although he claims Texas as his home and is a graduate of the University of Texas, he lives in Marietta, Georgia. Married to Liz, father to Jeffrey, Michael and Maddie, he has been well trained by his Chocolate Lab Chewie and Cairn Terrier Sasha.

For more information, visit
www.killingsustainability.com

69003759R00105

Made in the USA
Columbia, SC
18 August 2019